RUSH
SONG BY SONG

ALEX E. BODY

FONTHILL

First published in Great Britain in 2019 by Fonthill
Reprinted in 2026 by Fonthill
An imprint of
Pen & Sword Books Ltd
Yorkshire – Philadelphia

Copyright © Alex E. Body 2019, 2026

ISBN 978-1-78155-729-7

The right of Alex E. Body to be identified as Author of this work has been asserted by him in accordance with the Copyright, Designs and Patents Act 1988.

A CIP catalogue record for this book is available from the British Library.

All rights reserved. No part of this book may be reproduced, transmitted, downloaded, decompiled or reverse engineered in any form or by any means, electronic or mechanical including photocopying, recording or by any information storage and retrieval system, without permission from the Publisher in writing. NO AI TRAINING: Without in any way limiting the Author's and Publisher's exclusive rights under copyright, any use of this publication to "train" generative artificial intelligence (AI) technologies to generate text is expressly prohibited. The Author and Publisher reserve all rights to license uses of this work for generative AI training and development of machine learning language models.

The Publisher's authorised representative in the EU for product safety is Authorised Rep Compliance Ltd., Ground Floor, 71 Lower Baggot Street, Dublin D02 P593, Ireland.
www.arccompliance.com

For a complete list of Pen & Sword titles please contact

PEN & SWORD BOOKS LIMITED
47 Church Street, Barnsley, South Yorkshire, S70 2AS, England
E-mail: enquiries@pen-and-sword.co.uk
Website: www.pen-and-sword.co.uk
or
PEN AND SWORD BOOKS
1950 Lawrence Road, Havertown, PA 19083, USA
E-mail: uspen-and-sword@casematepublishers.com
Website: www.penandswordbooks.com

Foreword

Few bands in the history of rock music inspire such polarised opinion as Rush. From their modest beginnings as a blues rock cover band playing small bars in Toronto, Rush's career was built on the firm foundation of constant touring. Originally forming in 1968 as high school friends—guitarist Alex Lifeson, drummer John Rutsey, and singer and bassist Jeff Jones—it was not until 1971 that Geddy Lee would join the band, replacing Jones to create the original line-up. Rutsey would remain in the band until 1974 when he was replaced by Neil Peart, thus creating the definitive Rush line-up. Since 1974, Rush's line-up has not changed.

Even from their earliest days, the band developed and changed constantly, losing and gaining fans along the way—but famously retaining their integrity—always moving in the direction that they chose.

In this book, I have tried to follow the journey of Rush through their compositions, tracing the origins of some of the band's unexpected (and sometimes unpopular) changes of style, as well as highlighting the band's great achievements along the way. The writing is deliberately as objective as possible, although, due to the nature of music, this has not always been possible. Nevertheless, this is a book designed to reveal the inner workings and background behind the band's enormous repertoire; it is not a review of it.

Rush were known for many years as 'the world's biggest cult band'; indeed, with twenty-four gold records and fourteen platinum records, they are only succeeded by The Beatles and The Rolling Stones for the most consecutive gold or platinum studio albums by a rock band.

As the band's enormous influence on modern rock music became evident in the twenty-first century, Rush are now regarded by rock fans and musicians alike as one of the most important rock acts to ever come out of North America. After more than forty years of writing and touring, in 2017, it seems that the band may finally be at the end of their career. Rush fans, however, know that the only thing to expect from Rush is the unexpected.

Author's note: Given the stability of the band's line-up I have chosen not to list the line-up against each album. As a result, the reader should assume the line up to be, unless shown otherwise:

Geddy Lee: bass, vocals, keyboards
Alex Lifeson: guitars
Neil Peart: drums and percussion.

Acknowledgements

Thanks are due to Stephen Lambe for support and advice along the way. Alex Dunbar, Mitch Simpson, Sebastiaan van Stijn, and Tim Starace for their photographs and memorabilia, my mum and dad for 'getting the ball rolling', and Audrey for her enduring patience.

CONTENTS

Foreword		3
Acknowledgements		5
1	*Rush*	9
2	*Fly by Night*	16
3	*Caress of Steel*	23
4	*2112*	30
5	*A Farewell to Kings*	36
6	*Hemispheres*	41
7	*Permanent Waves*	46
8	*Moving Pictures*	52
9	*Signals*	59
10	*Grace Under Pressure*	67
11	*Power Windows*	73
12	*Hold Your Fire*	81
13	*Presto*	89
14	*Roll the Bones*	96
15	*Counterparts*	102
16	*Test for Echo*	108
17	*Vapor Trails*	114
18	*Snakes and Arrows*	123
19	*Clockwork Angels*	130
20	*Live Albums, Solo Albums, and Curiosities*	138
Endnotes		154
Bibliography		158

1

Rush

Release date: 1 March 1974
Current edition: Virgin / EMI CD
Personnel: John Rutsey—drums
Recorded at Toronto Sound Studios and Eastern Sound
Produced by Rush, remixed by Terry Brown
Chart position: Canada: 86
UK: Did not chart
US: 105

In 1973, Geddy Lee, Alex Lifeson, and John Rutsey recorded their eponymous album: *Rush*. Initially released in Canada on their own vanity label, Moon Records, the album was met with good local reception although the initial pressing of 3,500 units seemed ample.

However, shortly after the album's release in 1974, a Cleveland DJ, Donna Halper, added the song 'Working Man' to her regular playlist. This decision was arguably the single most important of Rush's career. Cleveland, a factory town, immediately took to the song, telephoning the station in droves whenever the song was played—often convinced that the track was a new Led Zeppelin single. This unexpected reaction led to the signing of Rush to the major label Mercury, which distributed the album in the USA and subsequently internationally—though not until some changes had been made.

The recording had initially been done on a tight budget with the band laying down tracks at Toronto's Eastern Sound on an outdated 8-track recorder. These sessions were done overnight during the studios 'dead' period to further reduce the financial outlay. Unhappy with the results, overdubs—and some new tracks—were recorded at Toronto Sound Studios where the band produced themselves and were happier with the result, but this was not the record Mercury wanted to put out. Rush's manager Ray Danniels agreed to fund the recruitment of Terry Brown to perform a remix. Brown would produce eight subsequent Rush albums and was often referred to as the band's fourth member. Another incredibly fortunate turn in Rush's career had just occurred.

This is the only Rush album on which original drummer John Rutsey performs. His solid rock drumming is a cornerstone of the original Rush sound, but, like many rock drummers of the time, he was reliable rather than spectacular. His musical interests leant more towards the traditional hard rock of the time, while Lee and Lifeson hoped to take their music into more progressive territory. It was, however, Rutsey's health that would eventually cause his split from the band. Unable to cope with an unforgiving touring schedule, his diabetes forced him to part ways with Rush.

This debut is often poorly reviewed by those who have written about it since the release of Rush's most popular material, and in the context of their other great work, this is understandable, but *Rush* is an energetic and exciting rock album that in 1974 deserved its enthusiastic praise.

Like almost every Rush album, their debut is an album that was hugely influenced by the musical styles that were in fashion at the time. On first listen, it is easy to dismiss this as another good but ultimately ordinary hard rock album. On closer inspection, however, there is much in this album that shows a band that have the potential to do great things.

While the album's lyrics do leave something to be desired, this is partially the responsibility of John Rutsey who was in fact the band's original lyricist. Shortly before entering the studio, Rutsey had a sudden lack of confidence in his work and ripped up the paper that his words were written on. With time short, it fell to Lee to write an album of lyrics in an extremely short space of time, or else waste the band's valuable studio time.[1]

The drumming on the album, though competent, lacks the inventiveness and style on display from the bass and guitar and so it is unsurprising that the album's two weakest points—the drumming and the lyrics—would, on the next album, be the responsibility of a new band member: Neil Peart.

Songs

'Finding My Way'
Alex Lifeson's distorted guitar slowly fades in interspersing huge Townshend-esque chords with a frantic three-note repeating lick. After a couple of measures, the listener is introduced to Geddy Lee's signature mid-70s wail. This vocal style, which came naturally to Lee, was described at the time by various critics as sounding like 'a hamster in overdrive', 'the dead howling in Hades', 'strangling a hamster', and 'a cat being chased out the door with a blow torch up its ass', but was also, more kindly (and quite understandably), compared to Robert Plant's high register.[2]

The bass tone here is, for the era, unusually crisp and has a 'twang' that, among Rush's 1974 contemporaries, could only be found growling out of John Entwistle's amplifiers. It is no secret that Rush were massively influenced by bands of the 'British invasion' and the first few seconds of this debut make that statement loud and clear. After the thrilling intro, the song becomes a more standard affair for the era—albeit one with an unusually punchy and energetic sound, especially for a trio.

The lyric to 'Finding my Way' is simple, but one of the more meaningful on the album. Lines like 'I've been here so long/Lost count of the years' speak of the impatient young man desperate to escape the small town life. This sentiment would later be expressed, on numerous occasions, far more eloquently by their future lyricist, Neil Peart.

On listening to 'Finding My Way' with a knowledge of Rush's entire discography, each member sounds much more like their influences than the musicians they would in time become: Lee playing bass like Jack Bruce and John Entwistle while singing like Robert Plant and Lifeson doing his best imitation of Jimmy Page and Pete Townshend.

'Need Some Love'

A punchy start to an upbeat song that is, in many ways, indistinguishable from the fare on offer from most other mid-70s hard rock bands. The lyrics are particularly unadventurous ('Ooh I need some love/I said I need some love/Ooh I need some love'), especially when compared to the ambitious work that would later define the band.

Here Rutsey sounds completely at home driving the song along and performing effective rock fills. It is perhaps telling that it is on the more straightforward tracks that this is most evident. On this track, Lee begins to hint at the exceptional bass playing he is capable of. Subtle melodic runs and intricate bass lines that are a world away from the root note plodding that listeners had come to expect from many rock bands. Lifeson delivers a punchy and energetic solo that has hints of the off-kilter style he would later become known for.

With a duration of two minutes and nineteen seconds, 'Need Some Love' is over before it is possible to be bored of it, but the song is probably not one many Rush fans would remark on.

'Take a Friend'

Another fade in here, but with an odd repeating riff of the type Rush would become famous for in later years. This intro is perhaps the most interesting part of this otherwise laid-back blues-rock tune. The intro is followed by an unmistakably Led Zeppelin inspired riff, which forms the basis of the verse. A cheerful melodic chorus lifts the song and Lifeson comfortably slots in his lead licks around Lee's now slightly more reserved vocals.

It is worth noting that, yet again, the song writing here is very lean: before the two-minute mark, we have already had an intro, two verses, and two choruses.

Although much of this album sounds initially similar to many other bands of the time, the song writing offers little opportunity for the listener to be bored. While other bands may stay with a theme for minutes at a time, even at this stage of their career, Rush seem keen to develop ideas quickly and move on—a strength that has stayed with them as songwriters throughout their long career.

As well as Lifeson's Zeppelin-esque riffing on 'Take a Friend', Lee's vocal develops into a crescendo of 'yeah-yeahs!', which are, deliberately or not, so obviously a style picked up from Robert Plant. The effect is absolutely hammered home, however, with some gratuitous use of tape-delay causing Geddy's counter-tenor to echo across the track before Lifeson's riffing begins again.

The lyric to 'Take a Friend' is another extremely simple one: the three verses are ostensibly the same piece of writing with just the phrasing changed. There are no deep metaphors or double meanings here: 'Take yourself a friend/Keep 'em 'til the end/Whether woman or man/It makes you feel so good'.

'Here Again'

A sullen, down tempo riff opens this moody track. Lee's crystal clear bass plays a neat run over Rutsey's laid-back drums as the singing begins. The vocal performance here gradually builds from its reserved beginnings to an impassioned shriek. This is one of the few times in the album where the budget constraints are evident; if they had been signed to a major label when recording this, perhaps such vocal performances could have been perfected before pressing. In any case, here we have a moment in time: three young musicians recording their debut LP, with Lee quite literally still finding his voice.

The lyric here is a little more interesting and certainly makes an attempt to transcend the far more pedestrian work that makes up the rest of the album: 'Yes, you know that the hardest part/Yes, I say it is to stay on top/On top of a world forever churning'.

Once again, although we are listening to what is essentially a prototype of Rush, this idea of constantly progressing is a theme that occurs time and time again both in the band's future lyrics and indeed has been expressed regularly by the band in interviews. It should perhaps not be surprising that this notion has made it into the band's work so early in their career.

The entire first half of the song is a brooding build up. Lifeson's compelling chord work and Lee's earnest singing successfully produces tension that has its worthy release after four minutes. Another simple drum fill takes the song into its uplifting chorus, which shows a maturity in composition unseen in the previous three tracks.

Lifeson's famously free and avant-garde lead style seems moderated and slightly stilted during the song's guitar solo finale; this is perhaps another example of a time when more studio time would have allowed the song's performances to be fine-tuned.

Clocking in at seven minutes and thirty-five seconds, this song could arguably have been trimmed. However, extended pieces would become a signature part of Rush's catalogue and experimentations with over-long songs at this early stage of their career may have directly led to the extraordinary compositions they would later produce.

'What You're Doing'

The second side of *Rush* opens with an immediate and arresting riff contrasting neatly with the down tempo end of the first side. The bass and guitar are in perfect unison here providing the huge rock sound Rush were famous for in their early days.

The lyrics here are a rehash of many 'stick it to the man'-type lyrics that were common place during the late '60s and early '70s, and although they do not quite say anything in particular, this youthful rebellious song, particularly with Lee's enthusiastic delivery, is very entertaining.

The most exciting thing about this song is the instrumental fills. Between the standard bluesy verses, all three musicians perform fast and intricate runs that elevate the song from an amusing blues-rock number into something thrilling. If you are listening to this album with knowledge of Rush's later work, 'What You're Doing' is probably the most easily identifiable as having the Rush sound.

It is also worth mentioning that the lead guitar work here seems far freer and more expressive than on the previous songs. The faster pace, heavier sound, and greater energy perhaps providing a better foundation for Lifeson to build his solos on.

'In the Mood'

While every other song on the album is a Lee and Lifeson collaboration, 'In the Mood' is a pure Geddy Lee composition.

A strong vocal melody counterpointed cleverly by Lifeson's riffs make for a memorable pop song. Understandable then that this is one of the few songs from Rush's debut that made regular appearances in Rush live sets well into their career—often as part of a medley in the encore.

Rutsey's drumming here is careful and precise with interesting fills and changes in dynamics. A short break into a Merseybeat during the guitar solo helps make this one of Rutsey's best performances on the album. Although in 1974 it was hard to consider Geddy Lee as a particularly accomplished lyricist, his decision to rhyme 'Late' with 'Eight' actually ended up gaining the band a decent regular bit of airplay.

The St Louis Classic Rock radio station KSHE would regularly play the song every Friday night at 7.45 p.m. in reference to the song's chorus: 'Hey baby, it's a quarter to eight/I feel I'm in the mood'.

Before and After

Layers of acoustic, electric and bass guitar open 'Before and After' to create a beautiful lush sound that is unique to this point in the album.

'Before and After' is the first recorded effort of Rush's style of linear songwriting. The tender opening to the song is gradually developed and builds to a dreamy apogee, which then, surprisingly, is abandoned for a complete change of direction. The subtle guitars are now gone and with a perfunctory snare roll we are back into heavy blues-rock territory once again.

The unison riffs are particularly pronounced here, weaving around Lee's vocals expertly, but the lyrics unfortunately are more of the same. This time an appeal to rescue a failing relationship in the midst of a feud. The chorus, typically, is one word repeated four times: 'yeah!'

The breakdown section later in the second half of the song is without question the most Led Zeppelin sounding moment in the album—a heavy riff stop-starts between huge, straightforward drums. Lifeson soon fills in the gaps with his best Jimmy Page impression and, in some ways surprisingly, it really works. With Lee's voice deluged in reverb and delay the song finishes with one final shriek: 'I said yeah yeah yeah yeah!'

'Working Man'

'Working Man' was the song that broke Rush. A song about the rigours of working an ordinary 9–5 job, day-in, day-out. The simple lyric is effective because it is so ambiguous—it could apply to just about anyone. This is perhaps why the population of Cleveland took to the song so enthusiastically.

The lyric does hide yet another subtle, yet important line: 'It seem's to me I could live my life/A lot better than I think I am'. Ambition, and desperation to progress, is a theme once again.

The idea of a song that is over seven minutes long being the single that successfully introduces a listening audience to a new band is so alien today, and yet it was, in those days, something Donna Halper as music director of WMMS ensured she did for her DJs. She was always on the look-out for what she called 'bathroom songs': 'I had to think about my DJs. I was always looking for long songs that were also good songs, so they [the DJs] could do what they had to do'.[3]

The dark, baleful intro to 'Working Man' is one of the heaviest moments on the album. Reminiscent of Black Sabbath, this proto-metal track moves through several parts. Lee's vocals here are once again much more melodic forgoing the blues wailing for some powerful, yet tuneful singing.

After the second chorus, a short bass solo ushers in Lifeson's most technical solo on the album. This is a solo that ebbs and flows with bizarre almost dissonant flourishes counterpointed with tightly performed melodic runs. This is the moment on the album when the listener is offered a glimpse into the future—seeing hints of the extraordinary lead guitar player that Lifeson will become.

After the solo a fast repeating riff is played by the bass and guitar again and again building up to a crescendos segue into the song's final verse. Although much of the song writing on the album shows a band in their early days, this is a thrilling, flawless moment of rock music that the band continued to perform in the same way, note for note, right up to their final tour.

Interesting Liner Notes

A special thanks 'to Donna Halper of WMMS in Cleveland for getting the ball rolling' has been included on every reprint of *Rush* since its re-release on the Mercury label. Advice to the listener is also included: 'For best results play at maximum volume'.

2

Fly by Night

Release date: 15 February 1975
Current edition: Virgin/EMI CD
Recorded at Toronto Sound Studios
Produced by Rush and Terry Brown, Assistant Engineer: John Woloschuk
Chart position: Canada: 9
UK: Did not chart
US: 113

After Rutsey's split from the band following the release of *Rush*, the band urgently needed to recruit a replacement. A live tour had been scheduled and they were now signed to Mercury Records—a major label. There was a wave of enthusiasm and excitement about the band, which, if not harnessed quickly, would be wasted. So Lee and Lifeson immediately set about finding a drummer who could perform and write the kind of heavy, technical music they were enthused by.

The story goes that after a long day auditioning drummer after drummer, Peart arrived in his mother's Ford Pinto with his drums stored in rubbish cans.

Lee, reminiscing on their first meeting, said his 'first impression was that he [Peart] was kinda goofy', while Lifeson remembered his first thoughts being 'God, he's not *nearly* cool enough to be in this band!'[1]

When Peart started playing, however, Lee and Lifeson were utterly convinced they had found the right person. Lifeson's initial concern gave way to awe: '… he pounded the crap out of those drums. He played like Keith Moon and John Bonham at the same time'. Only a fortnight later, the new line-up began their first full North American tour.

In February 1975, just eleven months after the release of their debut album, Rush released *Fly by Night*. This album marks an incredible progression in a very short space of time, which was surely catalysed by Peart's recruitment.

While Peart's drumming was superlative, Lee and Lifeson remarked while on tour that he was almost always passing his time by reading. Suggesting to him that if he was keen on reading that he may also be interested in writing, Peart revealed he already had several lyrics ready to use. Peart's intellectual and literary style was often regarded as verbose and pretentious, but as time has gone by, his lyrics have been appreciated as insightful and interesting works.

The production on *Fly by Night* is a step up from *Rush* as well. With Terry Brown at the helm to guide the young band through the studio environment, this album is a marked improvement with incredible clarity and excellent instrumental separation. The album, with its crisp and bright sound, also manages to successfully capture the energy of the band's performances.

Honing their musical skills through relentless touring, and writing new material during downtime in hotel rooms and sound-checks, it is not just the addition of Peart that makes this album a more impressive one. Lifeson is more confident and creative than ever, while Lee's bass playing is more adventurous and technically in a class of its own. With a drummer who would later be widely regarded as the world's greatest, Rush's line-up was now complete.

This album, if nothing else, established the band in their final form. In comparison to their debut, Lee and Lifeson were performing and writing with a new confidence and a sound that was much more their own. While certain influences (Led Zeppelin and The Who particularly) are impossible to ignore, this feels much more like an album of fresh music rather than a new band keen to emulate their heroes.

While this album is still enjoyed by many Rush fans, and rightly regarded as a great collection of songs, the second side of the album does lose a lot of energy after the relentless side one. While the album finishes on a high note with the brilliant 'In the End', the album's second side is a patchwork of rock and folk and would perhaps have been improved by an additional hard rock song.

In some ways, the fact that *Fly by Night* is more exploratory and progressive may explain why it did not produce the same critical excitement of the band's debut album. It also, to the disappointment of Mercury records, failed to produce a successful single.

Songs

'Anthem'

The crash of cymbals and growl of guitars open the album with an explosive and hyperactive riff. The guitar and bass double up in unison and tightly perform a rapid descending run while Peart practically performs a drum solo over them. This is clearly a band that have made impressive technical progress.

After being presented immediately with Peart's complex and busy drumming, the listener is suddenly presented with another huge change to the band: the lyrics. Whereas the songs on the previous album were largely typical hard-rock fare, 'Anthem' is a song inspired by Ayn Rand's controversial philosophy 'objectivism'.

Rand had written broadly on what she called 'the virtue of selfishness', and this song, about the importance of autonomy and self-determination, paraphrases Rand's points in a concise and effective way: 'Live for yourself … there's no one else/More worth living for/Begging hands and bleeding hearts will only cry out for more'.

Halfway through the song, one of Lee's incredibly high-pitched wails carries us into a guitar solo. Lifeson's guitar is fantastically lyrical here showing an ebb and flow in the composition of the solo and a player who has developed his own unique style—mixing the frenzied and frenetic with the restrained and melodic.

Beneath the guitar solo is the type of flowing and serpentine bass playing listeners had come to expect from Lee, and yet, the drums which had previously provided a mere foundation for this are now matching Lee beat for beat, fill for fill, and pulling the bass along into previously uncharted places. This is not just a guitar solo but a thrilling instrumental section.

Seamlessly leading from the solo into another verse, the song makes its final lyrical point: 'Well, I know they've always told you/Selfishness was wrong/Yet it was for me, not you, I came to write this song'.

'Best I Can'

Keith Moon's influence on Peart can immediately be heard at the beginning of this track. A busy, playful fill begins the song before leading into a repetitive chord progression interspersed with chromatic runs by the bass and guitar as well as numerous unusual drum fills. Listeners, at this point, will begin to realise that Peart's drum fills often start at unusual moments and rarely finish when expected. This is one of the reasons that a relatively simple rock song such as this is, in its final form, an impressive technical musical work.

This song was written before Peart's introduction into the band and footage does exist of Rush performing 'Best I Can' with John Rutsey. It is amazing the difference that Peart's incendiary drumming makes to a song that, otherwise, would not have sounded at all out of place on the first album.

One improvement here that Peart cannot take credit for is in the song's lyric. Lee's simple expression of the band's ambition is not overly sophisticated—'Rock and rollin's a scream/makin' millions my dream/Well, I do that a lot'—but this is surely part of the song's charm, and it is interesting to note that this is yet another song about ambition.

Lee's vocal delivery seems to have even more gravel here, and at times it does sound forced. While the enthusiastic delivery is enjoyable, his diction is poor, often making the lyric sheet a requirement whilst listening.

The use of a wah-wah pedal here is interesting, providing at times a huge treble boost somewhat comparable to Brian May's tone. His style, however, is entirely different—though no less confident. Lifeson here shows a command of his instrument and a real feel for melody in this short solo.

After another verse and some thundering displays of Peart's double-bass drumming, this lively song comes to an end. A song that bridges the gap between the straight-ahead rock of the debut album, and the more technical direction of the second.

'Beneath, Between and Behind'

During 1975, Rush spent a great deal of time on tour in the USA. It would have been impossible to miss the build up to one of the country's greatest ever national celebrations—its bicentenary. While the celebrations would not officially begin until 1976, many events occurred during 1975 and numerous works of art were commissioned. Although Peart was not commissioned to write this lyric, this is a relevant yet cynical observation on the state of the USA at the time, and what Peart saw as the corruption of the wishes of the founding fathers.

Peart shows the full force of his lyric writing ability here with this angry lament for the American dream and the band find a way to express the lyric musically in a punchy up-tempo song. The rhythm section of Lee and Peart sound perfectly connected here. Fills and stabs punctuate the song in a way that, despite their unusual placement in between bars, pulls the song along and draws the listener deeper. A groovy off-beat section, which foreshadows Rush's later fascination with reggae, is a surprising, yet welcome addition to the song.

'Beneath, Between and Behind' is an ambitious song, particularly lyrically, but it is successful. The lyric, despite its historical context, has remained relevant: 'The dream's gone stale, but still, let hope prevail/History's debt won't be repaid'.

'By-tor and the Snow Dog'

Back in 1974, Howard Ungerleider (who would still be working with the band forty years later) worked as tour manager, lighting director, and accountant for Rush. While spending time at the home of Rush manager, Ray Danniels, Ungerleider saw an altercation between two of Danniels' dogs—the more aggressive of the two, he called By-tor (biter), and the other small white animal, the Snow Dog. After recounting this story to the band, Peart wrote a lyric rather grander and more epic than the inspiration for it might merit.[2]

'By-tor and the Snow Dog' is arguably the first of the band's 'epics'. Although clocking in at a mere eight and a half minutes, it is the first Rush song to include programme-music and is the first of many fantasy inspired story songs.

The song couples a huge sounding production with a clarity that allows every note to be heard. Terry Brown's effect on the band's early sound can really be heard on this track.

The bi-amped growl of Lee's Rickenbacker takes us into the experimental mid-section of the song, which represents the battle between the devil-prince, By-tor and his nemesis the Snow Dog.

This instrumental passage is in four parts. The first section, 'Challenge and Defiance', is a powerful and up-beat heavy rock section where the battle is portrayed sonically. Lifeson represents the Snow Dog with a cacophonous screeching solo, while Geddy's growling bass, sounding somewhere between a pig and lion, portrays By-Tor. The next section '7/4 War Furor [*sic.*]' is a mind-melting composition of what would, in about twenty years' time be called 'math-rock'. With three drum solos (all, of course in 7/4) mixed up in a wild octave shifting pattern of enormous sounding bass and guitar unison, this section suddenly fades away as the battle draws to an end in the ambient 'Aftermath'.

After a short build-up of martial snare drumming and guitar swells, the final section, 'Hymn of Triumph', is introduced with a simple fill. Lifeson performs his bluesiest solo of the album, harking back to his exploits on their debut, but this time with more confidence to explore and an even greater command of his instrument.

At the close of the song some chimes can be heard for just a moment. As this was the final song on side one, the original vinyl would allow these chimes to continue infinitely as the needle slipped into an infinite groove.

'Fly by Night'

A cheerful guitar riff opens the album's title track. A song about the excitement of change and the importance of personal progress. This short piece is by far the closest thing to a pop song on the album and, unsurprisingly, was the lead single.

Despite its catchy melody and optimistic lyric, there are several things about this song that are distinctly un-poppy, all of which go some way to explaining why it only charted at No. 88 in 1975. Lee's bass is as busy as ever and Peart—though somewhat restrained here—cannot resist performing his energetic and busy fills all over this track. Adding pounding double bass drums to a pop song has rarely led to commercial success. Lifeson forgoes his normal distorted crunch, opting for a softer clean tone up until it seems he can no longer hold back and allows his squealing Gibson to come to the fore.

Although the song does not sound forced (as such), it is very easy to imagine this being a song that was composed as a simple pop song and changed beyond all recognition before being put to tape.

'Making Memories'

The softer feel of the album's second side continues here with another light-hearted track. Jangly acoustic guitars and a folky rhythmic feel fit perfectly with the song's lyrical content describing the trials and pleasures of life on tour.

By 1975, Rush were committed to a punishing schedule of touring, and this song, while positive, does give some impression of the relentlessness of the band's workload. Peart, in later years would be publicly open about his lack of enthusiasm for touring.

The American folk feel continues as Lifeson performs an energetic slide guitar solo in the second half of the song, and as the band loosens up into an improvisational jam on the song's groove, 'Making Memories' fades out before the three-minute mark.

'Rivendell'

'Rivendell' is an almost unbelievable change of pace for what has up to this point been an upbeat rock album. This music was written entirely by Lee, who plays classical guitar and sings in an uncharacteristic soft style, which is jarring in its difference.

Peart's lengthy lyric describes the beautiful Elven town of Rivendell—of J. R. R. Tolkien's Middle Earth. Although the lyric has its origin in fantasy, the song is a perfect lyrical counterpart to the album's previous song, describing the author's longing for rest and respite, despite an insatiable drive for adventure.

With its soft guitars, gentle singing, and repetitive structure, it is easy to compare this song to a lullaby. The song was recorded towards the end of the *Fly by Night* sessions, with the band exhausted from an unrelenting schedule. Lee has recounted in interviews that when sampling the final mix of 'Rivendell', by the end of the song, at least one band member would invariably be slumped in their chair in front of the mixing console asleep, much to the chagrin of producer Terry Brown who would be forced to listen to the whole thing yet again before gaining the bands seal of approval on the final mix.

While the song is not a poor composition, at nearly five minutes long and with little dynamic or melodic change, it is arguably over-long. However, the piece does segue perfectly into the next track, which adds to the impact of the album's finale.

'In the End'

After the tender end of the previous track, 'In the End' begins with more soft acoustic guitars. Lee, returning to his bass, once again performs with a gentle voice, though with a perceptible increase in energy. A change from the maudlin 'Rivendell'.

The first verse and chorus are performed with no drums and, knowing that this is the final track on the album, a flash of disappointment must have crossed the minds of many listeners when at about a minute and a half, the music fades away and the track seems to end.

With enormous power and clarity, Lifeson's distorted guitar explodes out of the song. The power of which must be psychologically amplified by the previous six minutes of quiet acoustic music. Peart is back as well and powers into the main body of the song with Lee's Rickenbacker back at its growling best. On the first album, Rush attempted a similar style of soft intro/heavy song with 'Before and After'. 'In the End' is a great example of a good idea perfectly realised after experimentation on a previous album.

The lyric, one of the more ambiguous on the album, was written by Lee and Lifeson and has been interpreted as a love song or perhaps a lament to the author's shortcomings. The final line of the song is perhaps the most pertinent. After an entire song, understanding how the object of the song is superior to the song's author, Lee sings: 'If I think like you think/It doesn't make my load much lighter'.

Interesting Liner Notes

Donna Halper is once again thanked here and Howard Ungerleider is credited for his inspirational story: 'By-Tor characters inspired by: Herns'. The liner notes also contain the following advice: 'FOR BEST RESULTS PLAY THIS ALBUM'.

3

Caress of Steel

Release date: 25 September 1975
Current edition: Virgin/EMI CD
Recorded at Toronto Sound Studios
Produced by Rush and Terry Brown, Engineered by Terry Brown
Chart position: Canada: 60
                  UK : Did not chart
                  US: 148

While *Fly by Night* was the first time Lee, Lifeson, and Peart recorded an album together, several songs from that album had existed before Peart joined the band. Thus, *Caress of Steel* is the first album that is a true collaboration by the trio.

With the material written with Rutsey expended, and emboldened by their astounding new drummer, Lee and Lifeson were finally free to push the boundaries of progressive music in ways they had never been able to before. On *Caress of Steel*, Peart, for the first time, writes all the lyrics on a Rush album and is given free rein to lyrically explore history and fantasy as he wishes.

As well as being the first full collaboration by Lee, Lifeson, and Peart, *Caress of Steel* is also the first time Rush would hire artist Hugh Syme to design the album sleeve. Syme would later go on to produce the art for every subsequent Rush album. The record sleeves for *Caress of Steel* were originally designed to be printed onto silver backing, thus giving the appearance of steel. However, a printing error caused the metallic design to appear a darker copper colour, thus ruining the effect. For reasons that have never been explained, this error was never rectified and even recent reissues of the album have the copper-coloured cover.

The album contains the exuberance and youthful spark of a debut, but does also have its pitfalls: perhaps overambitious in places and certainly a challenging listen for a traditional rock audience, which was reflected in its poor sales and dreadful critical reception.

The tour for the album suffered from poor ticket sales, which resulted in the band being unable to pay their road crew, or their own salaries. The disastrous run of shows was subsequently referred to as the 'down the tubes tour'.[1]

While some regard this album as a bloated and pretentious failure, it is regarded by many fans as a hidden gem. It is, though, a strange album. The first three tracks would not have felt out of place on *Fly by Night* and were a clear continuation of the style fans had grown to love. However, Rush made the decision to include two incredibly ambitious tracks: 'The Necromancer' and 'The Fountain of Lamneth'. Both are tracks that require time to appreciate and it was arguably because of this that the album was a commercial and critical disaster. Rush have, on numerous occasions, described the sense that at this point their career was coming to an end.

The album is excellently produced and shows yet another jump in quality for the band's musicianship. Lee's vocals are beginning to be more palatable (and easier to understand), Peart's drumming is thrilling and Lifeson's guitar is fantastically chameleonic in its ability to shift in mood and timbre. The songs while entertaining still have a feel of 'work-in-progress' about them.

Under tremendous pressure from their record company to produce a hit album with a hit single, before beginning work on their next album, the band had to decide between their career and their integrity.

Songs

'Bastille Day'

Lifeson's roaring guitar boldly begins this opening track, joined by frantic rhythmic stabs from Lee's growling Rickenbacker and Peart's typically punchy drums. After the complicated intro, the listener is treated to a fast paced heavy rock song with a fantastically melodic chorus.

Lee's yelping and wailing is arguably more intense than ever, and it is perhaps even more apparent due to the extraordinarily wordy lyric. Unfortunately, Lee's diction is very poor, and while his vocal delivery is energetic, the excellent lyric can only really be appreciated with the benefit of the lyric sheet.

With this lyric, Peart sums up, with largely historically accurate detail, the storming of the French Bastille in 1789, which led directly to the bloody French Revolution.

As the song ends with a huge three-part guitar harmony, it is clear the band are more confident than ever in the studio and have no qualms about overdubbing extra instruments, despite only ever performing as a three piece live. Recorded live material of this era is available, and the power and energy of the performances easily makes up for the loss of the overdubbed parts that listeners found on Rush's studio albums.

guitar joins the main riff creating a powerful and commanding sound, which ends suddenly, before the introduction of part three, 'Return of the Prince'.

As Peart's spoken piece introduces part three above Lifeson's jubilant guitar, the listener is introduced, once again, to Prince By-Tor, who on the *Fly by Night* album was described as 'centurion of evil' and 'devil prince'. It transpires that this once-evil prince has come to redeem himself and defeat the Necromancer. The uplifting guitar continues as Lee sings of the traveller's escape and By-Tor's victory. Lifeson once again showcases his lead guitar abilities as the triumphant finale fades out.

Neil Peart, asked about By-Tor's change of heart (from evil to good in the space of only one album) simply replied: 'I guess he's like all of us—sometimes good, and sometimes he's bad!'[5]

'The Fountain of Lamneth'

After twelve and a half minutes of progressive exuberance in 'The Necromancer', Rush's most ambitious song to date, this final track, which occupies the entire of side two, is longer and more complex still.

The song, in six parts, begins with 'In the Valley'. Lifeson uses his twelve-string acoustic guitar to great effect here, once again bringing to mind the huge influence Jimmy Page still played on his writing. The lyrics, which chronicle the entire life of the protagonist, begin simply. The short punctuated lines then grow in length as the protagonist grows from a baby into a child, indicating the protagonist's development. The young character is drawn towards a captivating mountain in the east, atop which sits 'The Fountain of Lamneth'. The character is determined to climb it and discover its secrets above all else.

After the Led Zeppelin-inspired light and shade of part one, with its pleasant guitar and triumphant riffs, comes the jarring second part of the song, 'Didacts and Narpets'. This part represents the rebellious and chaotic teenage years of the character. A frenzied Peart drum solo punctuated with Lee yelling almost unintelligible words makes up the whole of this short part. Peart described the piece in a 1991 interview with the Rush backstage club:

> Okay, I may have answered this before, but if not, the shouted words in that song represent an argument between Our Hero and the Didacts and Narpets—teachers and parents. I honestly can't remember what the actual words were, but they took up opposite positions like: 'Work! Live! Earn! Give!'[6]

Part three, 'No One at the Bridge', begins with an arpeggiated guitar piece that rolls and sways, much like the ship described in the lyric. The protagonist has now begun his quest. No reason is given, but the character's ship has been the subject of a mutiny. Lashed to the ship's mast and alone, the outlook is bleak. 'No One at the Bridge' really highlights Terry Brown's excellent production on this album. Open sonic spaces contrasted with the tight heavy sections create a real sense of light and shade. Lifeson's majestic Genesis-inspired guitar solo at the end of the piece gives the listener time to reflect on the lyric thus far as we head into the second half of this epic song.

As the sound of sea-gulls fades into silence, part four, 'Panacea', begins. The music for this part was written by Geddy Lee and is a clear development of the style he tried on 'Rivendell'. A softly plucked classical guitar and gentle singing open the piece as the lyric describes the confusion of the protagonist who has survived the wreckage of his ship. He quickly discovers a woman and falls in love, tempting him away from his dream with 'Gentle hands that promise me/Comfort through the years'. The temptation, however, is not enough, and the character decides to head off to pursue the mountain rather than stay and make a life with his companion. 'Panacea', if viewed as a song in its own right, is one of a very few love songs written by Peart. Characteristically for Peart, its ending is decidedly uncharacteristic of the love-song genre. 'Panacea' was later decried by Lifeson: 'It was an attempt at something that didn't really work out. It was ... innocent'.[7]

After the downbeat ending to 'Panacea', part five, 'Bacchus Plateau', fades in with a simple and joyous guitar riff. Bacchus, the Roman god of wine, the reason for the joy. This piece is possibly the most interesting part of the lyric because it is up-beat and happy, and yet the protagonist has abandoned his dream in favour of drink. He openly and carelessly accepts the futility of life. It is overtly stated that the protagonist has not just lost sight of what's important, but, in fact, of himself: 'Crimson misty memory/Hazy glimpse of me/Give me back my wonder/I've something more to give/I guess it doesn't matter/There's not much more to live'.

The meaning of the line 'Draw another goblet/From the cask of '43' has been debated by Rush fans for years. It would fit the lyric if it was an allusion to the fact that Albert Hofman first tested his new respiratory drug LSD in 1943. Some believe it is referencing a Spanish liquor Mirablis, which owing to its forty-three ingredients is known as 'Licor 43'. Some also believe it is referencing Ayn Rand's 'Class of '43'—a group of intellectuals who began to meet in this year. However, in 1976, Peart appeared to still hold Rand in high regard and so it is unlikely he would use her group as an example of a pointless distraction.

At the end of 'Bacchus Plateau', the protagonist appears to have given up on his dream. His life almost over, he seems to have accepted his fate and indeed his failure.

The final part, 'The Mountain', opens with the same musical theme as part one, recalling the character's youth. He has reached the final stretch of his journey and can hear the 'dancing waters' of the fountain. At last, he has reached his goal and achieved his dream. The music in part six is identical to that in part one, which may initially seem strange owing to the fact that the lyric is describing the hero achieving his life-long dream. However, listeners (arguably generous listeners) may consider that this works with the cyclical nature of the lyric: 'Like Old Sol' behind the mountain/I'll be coming up again'. The fundamental line in the song comes in this final section: 'Many journeys end here/But, the secret's told the same/Life is just a candle/And a dream must give it flame'.

A candle, of course, has no function without a flame, and yet once lit, it is consumed by it. It is a credit to Peart's lyric that Lee's diction throughout the final track is far improved. Whereas earlier songs in the album are arguably verbose and have lyrics that in some cases do not scan well at all, 'The Fountain of Lamneth' has a complex and meaningful lyric that fits the music perfectly. While the song's ambition is clear to any listener, the song is in truth six separate pieces that have been stitched together in the studio. Aside from the first and final part, there are no continuing musical themes and the parts are only connected by studio fades.

Interesting Liner Notes

Beneath the print of 'The Necromancer' lyric is the following Latin phrase: '*Terminat hora diem; terminat auctor opus*'. This phrase, meaning 'The hour finishes the day; the author finishes his work', concludes Christopher Marlow's play *Doctor Faustus*.

There are also no lyrics printed for the 'Didacts and Narpets' section of 'The Fountain of Lamneth'. The album is dedicated to the memory of Rod Serling, the creator and presenter of the famous television programme *The Twilight Zone*.

4

2112

Release date: 1 September 1976
Current edition: Virgin/EMI CD
Recorded at Toronto Sound Studios
Produced by Rush and Terry Brown, Engineered by Terry Brown
Chart position: Canada: 5
UK: Did not chart
US: 61

In late 1975, Rush were preparing to embark on their next studio album. The excitement that had buoyed them on previously to explore and progress with new musical ideas was this time replaced by a profound disappointment. *Caress of Steel*, which the band had been hugely proud of, had failed to break commercially, and the tour had been a financial disaster. The band's record company, and even some of their own friends and family, were now pushing them to change their musical direction to something more commercially viable. If only they could produce a hit, perhaps then the band would be able to enjoy creative freedom later on in their career. The band responded to this advice by doing the complete opposite.

Whatever decision they took, this album would be the one that made them or broke them. Knowing this very well may have been their last album together, Alex Lifeson explains:

> You know, that came from a different place, more from a place of defiance and anger that things were sort of going the way they were around us. So we were fighting back. There was a lot of pressure on us, from the record company and, to some degree, from management, to go back to our rock roots, make another *Rush* album. And we basically said, 'You know what? That's not what we're about.... If we go down, we're going to go down in flames.'[1]

The band's defiant response to the pressure they were under had resulted in an album that they were proud of, and a piece of music that was, up to this point, the most ambitious and exciting thing they had written. To the bands surprise, and delight, the album was a commercial success. Owing to this, the band were from this point onward able to exercise complete creative control over their own work, delivering future albums to the record company as-is, with the executives confident that, while they did not necessarily understand why, Rush had fans that would buy the music they were producing in huge numbers.

Hugh Syme's defiant 'star man' emblem would go on to be a defining image for the band, appearing on t-shirts, posters, and the band's own bass drum heads for years to come. It is fitting that it is this defiant image that became more associated with Rush than any other.

Peart's open admiration of Ayn Rand and her objectivist philosophy would cause the band some trouble on the coming tour, however. An infamous *NME* interview (which Peart claims is largely erroneous and dishonest) equated the band's philosophy to the words that horrifically greeted those taken to the concentration camp at Auschwitz '*arbeit macht frei*'—'work sets you free'.[2] Of course, Geddy Lee's parents *met* at Auschwitz and the band sarcastically remarked to future British interviewers that, yes, they were the only Nazi band with a Jewish bass player.[3]

Still, people were talking about the band, and fans were more enthused than ever. In a complete reversal of fortunes, the tour for *2112* was as successful as the tour for *Caress of Steel* had failed to be. Riding the wave of success, the band decided that the time was right to record their first live album: *All the World's a Stage*.

Songs

'2112'

The atonal whirl of synthesizers opens the title track, bringing to mind the futuristic dystopia of 'Megadon', which is described in further detail in the liner notes. Before long, the epic piece begins in earnest with symphonically arranged power chords. This is proto-metal in the style of Tchaikovsky. Lee and Peart are as hyperactive as ever with the bass and drums performing frantic fills around Lifeson's huge sounding guitar. Lifeson's lead guitar is as driving and powerful as that of any contemporary rock band, but it has the signature excitably-high-strung style that is unique to Lifeson. As the opening section draws to its conclusion, among the sound of explosions, Lifeson plays a couple of licks of Tchaikovsky's *1812 Overture*—perhaps to destroy any ambiguity in the song's title. 'The Overture', the first section of this seven-part piece, draws to a close with its sole lyric—a line from a psalm: 'And the meek shall inherit the earth'.

Part two, 'The Temples of Syrinx', is the by far the heaviest piece the band had recorded thus far. A simple, straightforward heavy metal tune with a raucous and angry energy. The lyric describes the rulers of Megadon—the Priests of the Temples of Syrinx. These leaders seem to be an amalgam of a communist council and religious pedagogues with their disdain of questioning and fanatical propaganda. It is interesting—particularly in the world that has become reality in the years since the song was written—that the temples of Syrinx are filled with, of all things, 'great computers'.

Reeling from the zealous introduction to the story's evil antagonists, part three, 'Discovery', begins with the soft trickle of a waterfall. An out-of-tune guitar is diffidently plucked as we hear Lifeson musically represent the protagonist's discovery of a musical instrument—something he has never seen or heard before. Within moments, the piece has developed into an uplifting duet of guitar and vocals in Rush's rarely discussed, occasional folky style. The protagonist realises he has found an amazing thing and naïvely decides to take the instrument to The Priests. The gentle 'Discovery' segues perfectly into part four, the grandiose 'Presentation'.

Beginning with enormous chords that would sound right at home on a The Who album, the piece's tidal wave of an introduction ebbs away into Lee's folk-rock vocals. The humble protagonist presents the guitar to the priests, enthusiastically extolling its beauty and potential. The priests, represented by Geddy's high-register shriek, respond negatively, describing it as 'just a waste of time'. Another verse of petition does nothing to help our hero's case and only angers the priests further. Lee's shape-shifting vocal delivery is excellent here and really highlights his development as a vocalist. As well as an improvement in diction and a greater range of musical colour to his voice, Lee and Peart seem to have, by this point in their career, cracked the ability to fit lyric and voice together. Whereas previous lyrics had sounded loquacious, Lee's now natural delivery add to the enjoyment of the vocal from a purely musical perspective, but also add a greater depth to the lyrics themselves. At the immediate end of this piece, as a musical representation of the protagonist's fury, 'The Temple of Syrinx' theme is repeated at a blistering pace. Lifeson performs a rage-filled solo that, with its ferocious intensity, is uniquely Lifeson, but an over-the-top treble boost and brisk shredding evokes thoughts of some of Brian May's heaviest lead guitar moments.

A ghostly guitar opens part five, 'Oracle: The Dream'. With all hope destroyed, the protagonist's last haven is in the escape of sleep. In his dream, the protagonist sees the world as it ought to be: led 'light years away', he sees civilisations of free men 'with hungry mind and open eyes'—the antithesis to the lessons taught by the priests. The Oracle reveals to the protagonist that these idyllic civilisations belong to an elder race who left the planet long ago. The Oracle then reveals that the elder race plans to return home: 'Home to tear the temples down/ Home to change!'

Awakened from his dream and back to reality, the sixth sorrowful part of the piece, 'Soliloquy', finds the main character at his lowest ebb. With no hope at all, and grieving for a seemingly impossible dream, he decides to commit suicide. Lifeson's forlorn guitar coupled with Lee's dejected vocals express the mood perfectly. While the song starts in a low-key and depressed style, as the protagonist's distress builds further, so does the song. Finally heralded by a bawling guitar solo, the character kills himself.

An upbeat hard rock 'Grand Finale' is the final part in this epic seven-part piece. A driving riff builds to an outro that, with hints of the 'Temples of Syrinx' theme among furious guitar soloing, musically describes a great battle. The famous final words of the song are spoken right at the end: 'Attention all planets of the solar federation/We have assumed control'. While this ending is ambiguous, it is fair to consider that the earlier reference to the Elder Race returning home was not just a dream, but the superior civilisation communicating its plans to a potential ally. Peart has stated in interviews that he intended the ending to be a happy one, representing the liberation of the Planets of the Solar Federation, and a deposition of the priests

Aside from the fantastic gall of the band deciding to open their album with this grandiose and ambitious epic, it is a pleasing piece because it is, in many objective ways, significantly better than the band's previous attempts at this sort of song writing. The lyrics flow, the story has an arc, and the vocals express the lyric brilliantly. The music is thematic and, while songs like 'The Fountain of Lamneth' may as well have just been a collection of separate songs stitched together in aid of a common lyrical theme, '2112' is unquestionably one piece. The parts flow together, they fit tonally and melodically, and they reference each other. Perhaps the band's impudence was not an act of pure rebellion, but of confidence.

'A Passage to Bangkok'

After the unadulterated intensity of side one, the second side of *2112* opens with a playful fantasy travelogue. 'The Oriental Riff', used by numerous bands at around this time is a slightly cheesy anachronism which arguably highlights the whimsical intent of the song.

The song references numerous exotic locations around the world where the narrator has travelled in search of 'a sample of their yield'. Some prudish fans have tried to excuse the song as a satire on the hippy drug tourism of the '60s and '70s, but this can be fairly easily discounted when one considers that all three members of Rush have, in various interviews, mentioned their occasional cannabis use at around that time. Terry Brown in fact revealed that careful listeners can hear audio evidence of this in the short build up before the guitar solo at around the one-minute and fifty-second-mark of the song.

While this laid-back and light-hearted song is a huge change of theme from side one's epic, the musical complexity is undiminished. The guitar solo section is a typical Rush instrumental that tricks the listener with its simple off-beat groove that every so often changes time signature. The guitar solo, of course, never obviously deviates from its apparently simple hard rock groove. This section is one of the few that Lee would perform live with a rhythm guitar—using his Rickenbacker double-neck and filling in the bass part with his Moog Taurus pedals.

'The Twilight Zone'

After his death in 1975, Rush, who were huge fans of *The Twilight Zone* television series, dedicated *Caress of Steel* to the memory of its creator, Rod Serling. Continuing with the light-hearted feel of side two, this song is about that famous programme. The shortest song on the album, 'The Twilight Zone' has what is, for Rush, a remarkably simple structure with little in the way of musical extravagance—focussing instead on atmosphere. While it is totally different in sound, this simple yet textural style of writing may owe much to songs that Rush would write much later in their career such as 'Witch Hunt' and 'Mystic Rhythms'.

The lyric deftly contracts two episodes of the programme into two short verses. The first verse is based on 'Will the Real Martian Please Stand Up?' in which a friendly diner employee is found to be a three-eyed alien. Verse two is about the episode 'Stopover in a Quiet Town', where a hungover couple find themselves the playthings of a gigantic little girl. Perhaps so he could more easily find a rhyme for 'toy', Peart makes one change to the story—making the giant child a boy.

Evidenced by the numerous textural overdubs, the band were clearly at home in the studio while recording this song. Aside from the various extra electric and acoustic guitars, Lee's vocals are doubled in the chorus with a subtly mixed second vocal whispering along to the main melody in what is an unsettling and initially inconspicuous addition, perfectly apposite for the song's subject.

'Lessons'

Notwithstanding the short solo acoustic guitar pieces that would come later, 'Lessons' is the only Rush song written entirely by Alex Lifeson. The song's acoustic guitar-driven verse relaxes the listener into the song before Pete Townshend's influence can be heard loud and clear once again in Lifeson's blasting power chords. The defiant sound of the album's first side returns in 'Lessons' as Lee shrieks through the chorus in the style he had adopted earlier when performing the part of the totalitarian Priests.

While it is not objectively poor, the ambiguous and slightly unwieldy lyric highlights just how good Peart's writing is. 'Lessons' is yet another Rush song about ambition and progress—showing gratitude to those who have helped along the way, but frustrated and exasperated with those who refuse to listen and understand the lessons that are offered to them.

The first side of the album was notable in its aggressive and rebellious defiance, and it has been said time after time that Rush refused to bow to the pressure exerted on them by their record company and peers. However, it is worth considering that by this point in the album, it is possible to think that some of the material on the second side was an attempt at compromise. While 'Lessons' is a very enjoyable rock song, it breaks little ground. A simple structure and short run time make it a fun, but ultimately inconsequential piece.

'Tears'

Following on from Lifeson's solo piece comes this mawkish effort from Geddy Lee. One of Rush's few love songs, it is notable as the first Rush song to feature keyboards in a musical role. It is also the first to feature a guest musician. While Geddy Lee would, in years to come, become a keen synth player, on this track, the unmistakable warble of a Mellotron is played by the band's graphic designer, Hugh Syme.

One criticism that has been levelled at Rush throughout their career is that while their music is technically excellent, there is little in the way of emotion or 'feel' in their music. This song appears to be an attempt to counter that criticism, but its over-sentimentality, with swelling strings and yearning vocal, sounds trite.

'Tears' is the album's most notable change—in tempo and timbre. It does also, by way of contrast, vastly increase the power of the albums next, and final, song.

'Something for Nothing'

After two solo pieces, we return to the band working again as a singular unit, and—arguably, more importantly—to Peart writing the lyrics. 'Something for Nothing' is a return to the Ayn Rand inspired objectivist lyrics of side one. According to Peart, he was inspired to write the song after passing a piece of graffiti stating the platitude 'Freedom isn't free'.

While many songs deal with the idea of fate being a benevolent force or that everything will turn out alright in the end, Peart totally refutes this idea—but in a completely positive way. Rather than waiting, perhaps in vain, for things to work out right, 'Something for Nothing' is a call to arms for everyone to make their own destiny and realise their own dreams by their own means: 'In your head is the answer/Let it guide you along/Let your heart be the anchor/And the beat of your own song'.

The music itself is a brilliant return to the fast-paced progressive hard rock of the album's first side. The bass here is particularly energetic with speeding runs and extra notes that really turn the bass into a lead instrument. The sheer power of this song is particularly impressive for a trio.

Interesting Liner Notes

As well as the lyrics to all the songs on the album, the liner notes include short introductions to each of the opening piece's sections in prose.

2112 also has the note: 'With acknowledgement to the genius of Rand'. This, however, is altered to 'genus' in the CD edition. This may be a typo, or it may be an attempt to limit the connection the band has to this controversial figure—a connection that still draws criticism today. There is also 'Special thanks to ... (insert your name here)'.

5

A Farewell to Kings

Release date: 1 September 1977
Current edition: Virgin/EMI CD
Recorded at Rockfield Studios, Wales
Produced by Rush and Terry Brown, Engineered by Pat Moran and Terry Brown
Chart position: Canada: 11
UK: 22
US: 33

With their collective confidence renewed by the positive reaction to their most recent tour, and the live recordings that were made of it, the band approached their fifth album with an independence that they had been unable to previously enjoy. While their four prior studio albums had been recorded at Toronto Sound Studios, *A Farewell to Kings* would be recorded in Rockfield Studios in Wales, and subsequently mixed at Advision Studios in London.

With the success of *2112*, the band were at last truly free to explore songwriting in any way they chose, and while *A Farewell to Kings* features a couple of longer progressive pieces, the overall style is focussed and punchy. It was, of course, this album that produced the band's first international hit single, 'Closer to the Heart'. It is also the first album in which Lee would begin to use a large number of synthesizers, a decision that would eventually become controversial among Rush fans.

After the success of *2112*, Rush were finally free to do exactly as they pleased. *A Farewell to Kings* is the first album where they were genuinely under no pressure to fit a mould or make a hit—this was Rush, unadulterated.

With a consistent sound the album fits together well without becoming monotonous. The lyrics, like the music, are on related but not identical themes.

The two longer pieces, 'Xanadu' and 'Cygnus X-1', each run to over ten minutes, but unlike previous lengthy efforts, they are succinct in their execution. They do not, as was arguably the case with *2112*, create the feel of an album of two barely related halves. Many consider this to be the first great Rush album and its consistency is surely a reason for this.

With an accidental hit in 'Closer to the Heart' and a growing legion of fans buying their records and concert tickets, this album marks the beginning of a confident upward trajectory that would mark the second chapter of the bands career.

Songs

'A Farewell to Kings'

Notwithstanding the short synthesized intro on *2112*, every Rush album to date had opened with the distorted blast of an electric guitar. Here, though, we hear the full influence of the British prog-rock movement on Rush. A delicately plucked classical guitar is the first sound to be heard on the album, and this is soon followed by a synthesizer melody that is emphasised by Peart's xylophone.

Just over a minute passes before the raw power of Rush is finally brought to bear in the form of an enormous descending chord progression, which, typical of Rush, subtly shifts in time signature.

Lee's vocals have all the power and energy that have become his trademark, but have a renewed precision. It sounds as if Peart's occasional verbosity as a lyricist is no longer a challenge to Lee, but an asset that makes the vocal performance even more interesting.

The lyric to this song is a damning indictment of the establishment and society of the time. Criticising the hypocrisy and greed of the powerful—the 'scheming demons dressed in kingly guise'. The masses are not left untarnished by Peart's venomous pen either, blaming the common man for his myopia and lack of engagement: 'We turned our gaze from the castles in the distance/Eyes cast down on the path of least resistance'.

After being so vilified by certain members of the press for their political views, it is interesting that while this song does continue with the theme of individuality and anti-collectivism, this song shows a lightness of touch when it discusses the subject of the balance between the 'heart' and mind—a subject that would be thoroughly explored on the first side of the band's next album. The lyric finishes with a self-reference to the third song on the album: 'Can't we find the minds to lead us closer to the heart?'

Clocking in at nearly six minutes, this opener to Rush's 'second chapter' covers a lot of musical ground in a relatively short time: a complex lyric, a shifting jazzy interlude, and the powerful hard rock that fans had come to love. It is an example of the efficient and punchy writing style that would eventually come to define the band, a style that foregoes none of the complexity or ambition of the progressive rock bands of the time, but that also manages to condense numerous ideas into short and powerful hard rock songs.

'Xanadu'

While spending enormous amounts of time couped up on the band's tour bus, Peart was known as a voracious reader. It is unsurprising then that so many literary works influenced his lyrics. Rather than being a mere influence, however, Xanadu is almost a retelling of the Samuel Taylor Coleridge poem, 'Kubla Khan'.

The song is notable for numerous reasons, not least because of its extravagant introduction that lasts almost half the length of the song. There is also probably no other Rush song in which each member performs on so many different instruments. Peart indulges in a huge array of unusual percussion, including temple blocks, glockenspiel, wind chimes, tubular bells, and a bell tree—as well as his substantial standard kit. Lee and Lifeson famously performed this song live each using their own double neck guitars—Lifeson with a Gibson EDS-1275 (a guitar on which each neck has twelve and six strings respectively) and Lee with his Rickenbacker 4080 (which consists of a four-string bass and six-string guitar). Lee and Lifeson also both played bass pedals, while Lee maintained his other duties of keyboards and vocals.

Despite its eleven-minute runtime, the song is another example of a huge number of musical ideas being executed in what is actually a relatively compact song. It is also another example of Rush's exploration of programme-music—the ethereal synthesizers bringing to mind Coleridge's imagined world of legendary palaces and immortality, while the racing guitars could represent the tireless quest for Xanadu itself.

Despite its unconventional structure and a running time that makes it virtually unheard on mainstream radio, 'Xanadu' is an extremely popular song among fans and was played live regularly; indeed, Lee and Lifeson brought out their double necks one final time to perform the song for their *R40* tour.

'Closer to the Heart'

Opening the second side of the album is one of the band's most popular songs. Charting at No. 36, this was the first Rush song to be a Top 40 single in the UK. The song is also the first Rush song that had lyrical contribution from an outside collaborator: Peter Talbot—a fellow musician and friend of Peart.

A companion piece to the album's opening track, this song suggests a solution to the corruption of the modern world and the disillusionment many feel about it. While the Ayn Rand-inspired ideas of independence and personal autonomy are still there, the song's ideas of each individual's role having equal importance, and the overall positivity of the lyric, make this much less controversial than some of Peart's earlier work.

Clocking in at under three minutes, it is a simple song with constantly shifting timbre. From Lifeson's crystalline twelve-string opening to Peart's use of tubular bells and glockenspiel right through to the exhilarating instrumental finale, the song covers an enormous amount of ground in a very short time.

After its success as a hit single, this song was played live at virtually every Rush concert up until it was dropped for most of 2002's *Vapor Trails* tour because (according to Neil Peart) 'we got sick of it'.[1]

'Cinderalla Man'

Geddy Lee was inspired to write this song after watching the 1936 Frank Capra film *Mr Deeds Goes to Town*, in which a the protagonist inherits a huge sum of money only to be declared insane after deciding to use the money to help the poor.

The song is arguably the strongest lyrical effort from Lee so far. While the piece is in some ways a perfunctory description of the film, it is certainly a more ambitious effort than the 'Need Some Love' style lyrics Lee had written on numerous occasions previously.

The song is another example of the rarely heard folky side of Rush. Led by Lee's strong melodic vocal and with an unusually laid-back chorus, both over Lifeson's strummed acoustic guitar, this piece is an enjoyable oddity.

Popular contemporary music styles have always found their way into Rush music and the mid-section of this song is a perfect example. Peart notes in the *A Farewell to Kings* tour book: 'This one features a very unusual (for us) middle instrumental section that might even be called (shudder) funky!'[2]

'Madrigal'

The shortest song on the album, 'Madrigal' is one of Peart's rare love songs. While the band were enjoying unprecedented success at this time, the sustained work-schedule began to take its toll. Between touring, writing, and recording, the time that the band spent with their young families was necessarily reduced.

Lee's delivery of this succinct piece conveys the weariness that the band must all have felt to some degree at this point. The dark imagery that begins the song is overcome by its assuredly optimistic end: 'In vain to search for honour/In vain to search for truth/But these things can still be given/Your love has shown me proof'.

'Madrigal' is remarkable as a Rush song for its simplicity of structure. A short verse is repeated twice with different lyrics and this is bookended by a short whistled melody on Lee's Mini Moog synthesizer. The song is without a frantic instrumental section, a change of time signature, and is even without a chorus. It is a simple love song in a tradition that goes back centuries. It is therefore understandable why the song was named after one of the oldest known western forms of this tradition.

'Cygnus X-1: Book I: The Voyage'

After the medieval allusions earlier in the album, this science-fiction-inspired song blasts the listener across the void of space towards a mysterious X-ray source.

Discovered by astronomers in 1964, the constellation of Cygnus holds in it one of the strongest cosmic X-ray sources detectable on earth. At the time of the song's composition, it was postulated that the source of these rays was a black hole, and as time has gone on, overwhelming evidence has been found to back up this theory, thus keeping the song's story at least somewhat rooted in reality.

Opening with a cryptic passage spoken by the band's producer, Terry Brown, the song's lengthy introduction gradually introduces a syncopated solo bass line, which subtly changes time signature with every repeat. The amorphous space-rock intro is suddenly transformed into a tight and crisp math-rock riff, which is repeated by all three members of the band. This famous riff has often been used by the band as a medley section or outro in live shows since.

The lyric covers common ground for Rush. It is another story of an ambitious explorer. The quest this time is extra-terrestrial however, an interstellar voyage. The explorer's ship is named the *Rocinante*—after Don Quixote's horse in the eponymous novel. In a clever piece of foreshadowing (or a stroke of luck), the horse, Rocinante, was so named because it etymologically describes a former nag that is now a magnificent steed; the sequel to this song (opening the next album) describes the protagonist's own transformation.

After flying through space towards the irresistible call of the X-ray, the song finishes with a spectacularly cinematic section—the protagonist and his ship utterly destroyed as Lee shrieks: 'Sound and fury/Drowns my heart/Every nerve/Is torn apart'.

The former ubiquity of Lee's shrieking caused the style to lose much of its impact. The subtler vocal performances on this album lend this vocal finale a power that it would otherwise have lacked. This is Rush learning the art of composing programme-music, and excelling in its execution.

As the roaring finale fades, mysterious chords slowly repeat again and again, gradually fading. Listening carefully to this quiet outro is worthwhile, however. Almost imperceptibly quiet, a faint heartbeat thumps away behind the chords. The album is over, but the story is not.

Interesting Liner Notes

Surely, for fans, the most tantalising notes in the album booklet are the three words at the end of 'Cygnus X-1': 'To be continued'.

A self-congratulatory thank you is made to 'Dirk, Lerxt, and Pratt'. These names are, of course, nicknames for each of the band members, Lee, Lifeson and Peart respectively.

There are two notable omissions from the liner notes: 'Xanadu' and 'Cinderella Man'. While both are based on other works, no mention of 'Kubla Khan' or *Mr Deeds Goes to Town* is made.

The album is finally 'Dedicated to Nancy, Charlene and Jacqueline', the band members' wives.

Hemispheres

Release date: 29 October 1978
Current edition: Virgin/EMI CD
Recorded at Rockfield Studios, Wales and Advison Studios, London
Produced by Rush and Terry Brown, Engineered by Pat Moran
Engineer (Mixing): Terry Brown and John Brand
Engineer (Vocals): Declan O'Doherty
Chart position: Canada: 14
UK: 14
US: 47

Released just a year after *A Farewell to Kings*, *Hemispheres* finds the band at the zenith of their progressive-rock era.

Recorded, once again, at Rockfield Studios in Wales, the album's production retains the clarity of *A Farewell to Kings* but has an added power that, with its challenging material, makes the album significantly more accessible to rock fans than it otherwise might have been.

Confidently continuing in their own direction, the band are clearly pushing the boundaries with the music they can write and, indeed, play. Terry Brown once stated in an interview that in the hurried recording sessions they had inadvertently written (and recorded) music, which had to be sung in such high pitch that Lee's vocals were extremely difficult to successfully perform. The music itself is extraordinarily complex, taking numerous attempts to record a good take.

With only four tracks on the album, including a multi-part, single side epic and a nine-and-a-half-minute instrumental subtitled 'An Exercise in Self-Indulgence', if any further evidence were needed that Rush were going their own way, this is it.

The experiments that made *A Farewell to Kings* such a colourful album have, in *Hemispheres*, been carefully distilled into what is arguably Rush's most confident album so far. Lyrically, it is a clear progression from the anger and frustration of Peart's earlier work on *2112*, and this album, as well as clearly aiming to entertain, seems to show a keenness to illuminate rather than evangelise. In one sense,

Hemispheres showed an immense maturity in the band—and yet the music carries with it a rare exuberance that shows a joyful rejection of precedence. As the last album Rush would release in the 1970s, the album marks the end of the band's 'progressive-rock' era. While their music would continue to be 'progressive' in the true sense, many of the tropes of nominal prog-rock would never be repeated in such grand fashion by the band. The complex approach to songwriting that makes *Hemispheres* so popular among prog fans would, however, continue to be surreptitiously used for the rest of their career, even in their most popular and accessible songs.

Songs

'Cygnus X-1 Book II: Hemispheres'

After courting controversy with their attachment to some of Ayn Rand's philosophical ideas, this single-side composition is based on the work of another tendentious author: Friedrich Nietzsche. The work it is based on, *The Birth of Tragedy from the Spirit of Music*, claims that man's self-understanding is achievable through art, and most effectively through music.

Part one of the piece, 'Prelude', an overture, opens with an unusual and subtly dissonant chord, described by fans and musicians simply as 'The Hemispheres Chord'. Lifeson further cements his place as a unique guitar player in a single moment.

The piece moves deftly through numerous themes, which are heard again later in the song. With a short opening lyric, the scene is set for the epic nature of the song: a world divided between those who favour the god of love, and those who favour the god of reason. The tightly composed nature of this song reveals a gulf between the band's blues based jam songs and this pinnacle of progressive technicality.

Part two, 'Apollo (Bringer of Wisdom)', introduces Nietzsche's idea of the Apollonian—that is, the side of man that is concerned with reason, logic, and order. The population, excited to follow the path set out by Apollo produce all the finery of civilisation, build cities and discuss wisdom. However, after a time, the people question their motives. The once bustling cities fall silent and the populace decide to abandon Apollo in favour of his opposing counterpart, Dionysus.

Following Dionysus, the people concern themselves only with the sensual and spontaneous aspects of their nature. Part three, 'Dionysus (Bringer of Love)', is musically similar to part two, though this time following a contrary, though equally extreme philosophy. It is worth noting that although the god represented here makes sense within the story, the 'real' Dionysus was in fact the god of wine, rather than love. As in the preceding segment, after adopting their new way of life, the people enjoy themselves for a time. However, having abandoned their cities for the starry nights of the forest, a cruel winter destroys their impractical lifestyle and starvation ensues.

A powerful groove is jarred by an unusual time signature in part four, 'Armageddon (The Battle of Heart and Mind)'. The jarring repeating pattern seems an appropriate musical motif to represent the confusion and fear after the fracture of this story's society. The lyric goes on to describe the 'troubled years' of aimlessness that would follow this division until a small group begin to reveal the connection that this song has to its immediate predecessor—the legend of the Rocinante—and how it would travel to join them in their world.

Cleverly linking the two parts of 'Cygnus X-1', part four, 'Cygnus (Bringer of Balance)', begins with the same ascending scale that preceded the adventurer's entrance into the black hole in 'Book One'. The longest individual section of the whole piece, this is arguably the most sonically contrasting. Samples from 'Book One' are quietly played above a disconcerting ghostly synthesizer. The listener finds the adventurer immediately after his ship's and his own body's destruction—now a disembodied spirit who has found himself in the immortal realm of Olympus, the home of the gods. Looking down on the warring planet with sadness, his 'silent scream' is heard by the gods and the warriors below. At last, the ethereal synthesizer gives way to a blast of the powerful hard rock that has coloured the rest of the piece. The adventurer explains what he has seen and, after a period of contemplation, the gods appoint the disembodied man as one of their own, a mediator and peacemaker. Concluding this section, they turn to him and say: 'We will call you Cygnus/The god of balance you shall be'.

After a musical finale befitting this single-side epic—as an unexpected postscript—the sixth and final part of the song, 'The Sphere (A Kind of Dream)', begins with a softly strummed acoustic guitar. This section, lasting only a minute or so, underlines the meaning of the song and pressing the importance of balance and unity: of heart and mind, of reason and emotion. Peart puts it succinctly with this line: 'Sensibility armed with sense and liberty'.

This piece was Rush's last single-side track, and while it is comparable in many ways to '2112' and, in some respects, 'The Fountain of Lamneth', the two prior stories were in many respects quite simple. The complexity of this lyric is impressive, particularly when the literary and philosophical allusions are looked into with more depth. Musically, this is surely Rush at the height of their progressive-rock-era powers.

'Circumstances'

After the extravagance of side one, the second side of *Hemispheres* opens with this short and powerful proto-metal track. As the song moves through numerous complex riffs with the band almost constantly in unison, it is clear that Rush's heavier sound has developed hugely since the early blues-rock era. Whereas previous compositions had a huge amount of room for improvisation and extended soloing, this song is a good example of the tightly composed proto-metal that was a signature sound for Rush at this time.

The lyric, like the song itself, is short and to the point. It briefly describes the disappointment and disillusionment that Peart had felt as a struggling musician before joining Rush. As a young drummer, he had travelled to London in search of success, but failed to make any progress at all and found himself selling memorabilia to tourists to get by. Despite this apparent waste of time, success followed in an unexpected away, with Rush, and this is described in the second verse. While the lyric doesn't defer the responsibility for success entirely to fate, Peart's lyric expresses the importance of taking chances that are available, even though things will, in all probability, turn out far differently than expected.

'The Trees'

The B-side to 'Circumstances' when it was released as a single, 'The Trees' went on to be an extremely successful song in comparison, making it onto numerous Rush compilation albums and becoming a staple of the band's live sets.

Seamlessly shifting through different time signatures and timbres, this song successfully incorporates several different ideas into one relatively short piece of music in a way that few other bands would attempt.

The quiet introduction featuring Lifeson's classical guitar, Lee's melodic bass, and a sample of singing birds is soon blasted away by a powerful rock section that would not sound out of place on a The Who album. With its strong melody, the song remains musically interesting by switching between the heavy guitar of the verse and the bass-led chorus—each section switching between 4/4 (common) and 6/4 time signatures respectively. The atmospheric instrumental section features yet another time change and creates an appropriate aural picture of the embattled forest without over-developing the theme.

This song's lyric has been controversial for numerous reasons. While talking about the song, Peart explained: 'I was working on an entirely different thing when I saw a cartoon picture of these trees carrying on like fools. I thought, "What if trees acted like people?" So I saw it as a cartoon really, and wrote it that way'.[1]

The lyric describes the conflict between the large oak trees and smaller maple trees. The maples, unhappy that the oaks are able to 'grab up all the light', form a union and ensure henceforth that 'The trees are all kept equal/By hatchet, axe, and saw'.

While Peart is often hesitant to discuss the specifics of his lyrics, numerous fans have decided to interpret this lyric in different ways—usually depending on their own political views. The US Senator Rand Paul regularly quoted from 'The Trees' using the lyric as an allegory for the ills of state intervention. Keen to avoid any political association, the band sent a cease-and-desist order to Paul insisting that he stopped quoting the song.[2]

Some see the lyric as promoting a society in which there is equality of outcome, rather than of opportunity—this seems such a radical change from the objectivist philosophy that Peart was (in 1978) so recently enthusiastic about that it is almost impossible to believe. While the lyric is presented in a much more light-hearted way, 'The Trees' appears to fit with other anti-collectivist Peart lyrics such as '2112' and 'Something for Nothing'.

'La Villa Strangiato'

The fourth and final track on *Hemispheres*, 'La Villa Strangiato' is Rush's first solely instrumental track and is widely regarded as one of their most ambitious and impressive pieces. Running at just over nine minutes and split into twelve parts, the piece was apparently inspired by vivid dreams (or nightmares) experienced by Lifeson. Geddy Lee was, on occasion, equally disturbed by these dreams: 'Alex doesn't really call them nightmares. They're just strange dreams. He's plagued with them and he drives us crazy by calling us up all the time to tell us about them until we just say "Stop, you're giving me a headache."'[3]

'La Villa Strangiato' is an apt title for this wildly shifting piece that encompasses hard rock, jazz, big band, and cartoon music. While numerous people have accused Rush of pretentiousness in this era, it is almost unbelievable that a band would create music like this in an attempt to appeal to anything other than their own tastes; the piece is, after all, subtitled 'An exercise in self-indulgence'.

So ambitious was this piece that after countless attempts to record it in one take, the band finally relented and split the take into three. Lee has remarked that Rush spent more time recording 'La Villa Strangiato' than they did recording the entire *Fly by Night* album.

The repeating jazzy pattern that is known as 'Monsters' is a stylised approximation of another piece called 'Powerhouse' by Raymond Scott. This piece was used in numerous Warner Brothers cartoons and is, to this day, a staple piece for the use of cartoon animators. Rush did not initially credit Scott for the use of the piece and, years later, Scott's estate requested recompense from the band. By this time, however, the statute of limitations had expired and the band had no requirement to pay—though, to their credit, the band chose to make a 'penance' payment to his estate.

'La Villa Strangiato' was a regular part of Rush set lists and was a piece that was regularly toyed with. It has on various separate occasions had added to it: nonsense lyrics, a stream of consciousness rant by Lifeson, and a polka-style introduction.

Interesting Liner Notes

Readers interested in technical aspects of the album's production will be interested to know that 'This album was processed through the Duffoscope!'

As well as numerous amusing nicknames, the liner notes includes a long list of thank-yous. Notably to a few bands that Rush would become well known for touring with, including The Max Websters and The UFOs.

Permanent Waves

Release date: 14 January 1980
Current edition: Virgin/EMI CD
Recorded at Le Studio, Morin Heights, Quebec
Additional musicians: Hugh Syme—piano on 'Different Strings'
                               Erwig Chuapchuaduah—steel drums
Produced by Rush and Terry Brown, Engineered by Paul Northfield
Engineer (Mixing): Terry Brown
Chart position: Canada: 3
                           UK: 3
                           US: 4

Released on 1 January 1 1980, *Permanent Waves* is an album that builds upon everything Rush have done before, but for the first time is heavily influenced by modern mainstream pop music. This is the first album since *2112* that was recorded in the band's native Canada—at the legendary Le Studio. While the two preceding albums show a strong influence from the British prog-rock scene, this album exhibits a much stronger tendency to the popular brand of American hard rock of the time. While the band still had huge achievements ahead of them, songs like 'Freewill' and 'The Spirit of Radio' are, to this day, staples of hard rock radio as well as regularly being found on rock compilations. While Rush were already big hitters in the world of progressive-rock and metal, *Permanent Waves* marks their tentative entry into the mainstream.

At just over thirty-five minutes, *Permanent Waves* is Rush's shortest album, but it covers a huge amount of ground despite this. The forays into cinematic programme-music as well as the clear introduction of more contemporary pop sound began here.

The heavy reliance on keyboards and the more traditional approach to composition was controversial among many Rush fans, and despite selling well, *Permanent Waves* was not widely loved by fans, at least immediately after release.

It is now regarded as a seminal work and tracks such as 'The Spirit of Radio', 'Freewill', and 'Natural Science' have gone on to be fan favourites and have all continued to be played live more than thirty years after their composition.

Songs

'The Spirit of Radio'

The rapid repeating guitar riff that opens the song (supposedly designed to mimic the sound of radio static) provides an immediacy to this opener that hasn't been evident since *Caress of Steel*.

The song's lyric—which laments the demise of free and creative radio in favour of the overly commercial homogeneous medium it had become—was arranged musically in an attempt to give the impression of switching through various stations. In this relatively short song, the listener can hear rock, Mersey beat, prog (in the form of a subtle shift in time signature halfway through the song) reggae, and, for the first time from Rush, new-wave electronic music.

The song's title was the slogan of a popular Toronto radio station, CFNY (now known as Edge). The station's difficult history was part of Peart's inspiration for the lyric.

While the lyric is largely positive, praising the virtues of radio, the final section of the song parodies Simon and Garfunkel's 'The Sound of Silence'. A cursory glance at the lyric sheet reveals that the words of the 'prophets' now in fact read 'profits'. The concert hall that 'echoes with the sound of salesmen' is perhaps a reference to some of the many commercially focussed bands that Rush continued to tour with at this time. Bands that perhaps focussed so much on their own commercial success that it damaged their artistic integrity. The song remains the band's highest-charting single in the UK—peaking at No. 13.

'Freewill'

The songwriting tools that Rush had so far spent their career fashioning are used to great effect in this complicated, yet accessible song. Rush's ability to incorporate unconventional time signatures in a subtle way is a characteristic that is arguably unsurpassed by any other band; this song is a convincing testament to this.

The song's unorthodox verse is supported by a memorable melody, and where previous Rush songs may have sprawled out into bizarre musical outlands, this song is rooted in its simple chorus that verges on radio friendly pop rock.

After the song's second chorus, however, it moves into a bridge section that features musical pyrotechnics so condensed and distilled that, even by Rush's standards, this instrumental section is intense. The bass and drums perform a frenzied jazz-infused duet that would stand alone even without Lifeson's inimitable manic guitar that is the focus of this section.

Peart's maturation as a lyricist is further evidenced with the layered meaning of this song. With its violent imagery, the song warns of blindly following a particular tradition or ideology, while at once stating the importance of shaping one's own destiny. The increasing trend of philosophical fatalism is utterly rejected here. While songs like 'Something for Nothing' encourage the listener to shape their own destiny, 'Freewill' is a song that goes back a step in order to tell the listener that they actually can.

'Jacob's Ladder'

With its continually changing time signatures and linear composition, 'Jacob's Ladder' is a song that would not have sounded out of place on *Hemispheres*. However, the cinematic nature of the song, being one of the first full songs of programme-music that Rush would produce, is a hint of what was to come on the band's following album, *Moving Pictures*.

The song began life as an instrumental, with the band experimenting with textures and rhythms to build an aural panorama of brooding thunderclouds, before they break apart to form the meteorological phenomenon mentioned in the title. Unusually, Peart took a deliberately understated approach with the lyrics as, he describes here: 'We created all the music first to summon up an image—the effect of Jacob's Ladder—and paint the picture, with the lyrics added, just as a sort of little detail, later, to make it more descriptive.'[1] While this piece contains an enormous number of individual ideas, the song rapidly moves from one section to another. While previous efforts, similar in nature, may have occupied an album's entire side, 'Jacob's Ladder' was heavily developed and crafted ahead of its recording, being performed in various embryonic stages at several live shows. This was a luxury that Rush had rarely enjoyed previously and is perhaps part of the reason Rush were able to develop their sound so radically at this point in their career.

'Entre Nous'

The third and final single of *Permanent Waves* opens the second side of the album. Musically, the song is another change of direction for Rush with a tightly contained arrangement that places the vocal melody neatly at the fore while the other instruments decorate and support it.

Probably the poppiest song Rush had recorded to date, this song does not feature a guitar solo or any jarring changes. It is a testament to Rush's continuing maturation as songwriters. Many fans, however, objected to the taming of the band that had once been pioneers of the heavy metal movement.

The title (French for 'Between Us') was a widely used phrase in Ayn Rand's *The Fountainhead*—appositely, Peart's lyric once again alludes to the individual. He makes the point that even in our closest relationships our individual differences can remain hidden—secrets to be discovered. The song suggests this may be a positive point. 'Each one's life a novel no-one else has read' is perhaps a more exciting prospect than the one-size-fits-all love songs that have found themselves occupying the airwaves for decades. This is a song that recognises and celebrates individuality, and the need to grow as an individual.

Aside from his manic and sometimes atonal lead-guitar performances, Lifeson's other leading characteristic as a guitarist is his use of texture and arpeggiation to colour a piece. This is exemplified here in his work with the twelve-string acoustic during the chorus and the warm and detailed arrangement of the song's instrumental section.

'Different Strings'

Like 'Madrigal' from *A Farewell to Kings*, 'Different Strings' is a delicate song that was written, unlike the vast majority of Rush songs, to be played only on record.

A companion piece to 'Entre Nous', the lyric delves a little bit deeper and explains that, despite all our differences in sensibility, perception, and experience, we do share fundamental characteristics that we can all relate to: 'It's a part of us to be found within a song'.

Rush's long term artistic collaborator, Hugh Syme, makes another guest appearance on this track, performing the song's piano part.

'Different Strings' is the album's shortest and simplest song—a simple verse and chorus affair. However, the song features a yearning guitar solo from Lifeson, which, while widely regarded as an amazing piece of guitar playing, is criticised for its abrupt fade out just as the solo appears to be reaching its zenith. Lifeson is proud of the solo regardless: 'I love the feel of the tune. It reminds me of soldiers sitting around a piano in a smoke-filled pub in England during the war. It's the type of solo I really enjoy playing, an emotive, bluesy sort of thing'.[2]

'Natural Science'

During the preproduction process of *Permanent Waves*, the band found themselves with five fully completed songs, recorded as demos and nearly ready to commit to tape for the final album recording. However, the plan had always been to record a longer more progressive piece to finish the album—and this piece was not coming easily.

Peart had completed a lyric relating to the story *Sir Gawain and the Green Knight* (part of the King Arthur legend) and bits and pieces of music had been developed for it. The music, however, was never finished. The lyrical theme seemed so far removed from the new modern direction the band were forging for themselves that it was decided to scrap the idea and write something fresh. While his colleagues added final overdubs to the earlier demos, Peart sat alone with blank sheets of paper waiting for inspiration to strike.

After three frustrating days, the lyrics with their multiple themes and grand imagery came suddenly to Peart who refined them into three distinct sections.

At just over nine minutes, this song is relatively short in comparison to other songs in Rush's catalogue that are described as 'epics', yet this is just more evidence of Rush's continual effort to make their songs leaner—distilling them to their fundamental parts and removing the excess. 'Natural Science' is an ambitious and complex piece of music that is a favourite of fans and the band themselves.

The first section 'Tide Pools' opens with the sound of trickling water. This effect was created by Peart and Lifeson as they dipped oars into the lake outside Le Studio. Lee's gentle vocal joins Lifeson's acoustic twelve-string as Peart's lyric describes a microcosm of our individual universes—the creatures in tide pools that know nothing of their nearby neighbours—finding it impossible to imagine anything more 'Living in their pools/They soon forget about the sea'.

The scientific concept of 'Hyperspace' is space consisting of more than three dimensions. It is this concept that gives its name to the second part of the song. Reverse-reverb applied to Lee's vocals and a subtle shift in time signature to the final bar of each measure help this section to create a sense of the amorphous and multi-dimensional. The lyric describes the aforementioned microcosm's 'quantum leap forward' and, through implication, says that, far from being separate from nature and the universe, humanity is necessarily merely a part of the whole: '… the universe learned to expand'. Mechanised, computerised, synthetic science is being used to replace mankind rather than aid it.

The guitar solo that is performed at the tail end of the 'Hyperspace' section is a brilliant example of the unique lead-guitar style that Lifeson had developed by this point. Opening with almost dissonant harmonics, it develops melodically into a rage of speeding blues licks that with their careful and deliberate phrasing are uniquely Lifeson's.

The song's final part, 'Permanent Waves' offers a hopeful conclusion. Buoyed by yet another upbeat pop rhythm, the lyric compares science and nature—both must be tamed in an effort to preserve them. The theme of integrity, and its importance, is considered again: 'The most endangered species/The honest man/Will still survive annihilation'.

The 'permanent waves' that are alluded to in this part of the song and the album's title represent the cyclical nature of all things—as the tide pulls in, it will destroy all the previous tide pools, and yet, as it recedes, more will be created in their place 'Leaving life to go on/As it was'.

Interesting Liner Notes

As well as Hugh Syme's credit for playing piano on 'Different Strings', Daisy the Dog was credited as providing 'inspiration and vocal coaching'. In addition, Erwig Chuapchuaduah was credited for playing the steel drums.

Among the numerous and typical list of nicknames, 'Honourable mentions' are given to *Volleyball*, *Space Invaders* (10p), Euchre, Malibu, Grand Prix, *Hockey*, *M*A*S*H*, and Ho-Hooo!

The liner notes to *Permanent Waves* contained several mistakes on early releases of the album. Firstly, credit was given to Lee for the lyric to 'Different Strings', despite all the album's lyrics being written by Peart. Also probably the most well-known mistake is the misprint of the lyric to 'Freewill'. While Lee sings 'If you choose not to decide/You still have made a choice', the original lyric sheet reads 'If you choose not to decide/You cannot have made a choice'. Peart once responded to a question about this in a 1985 *Backstage Club Newsletter*:

> That's a funny question. I've had a few lately from people who are so sure that what they hear is correct, that they disbelieve what I've put in the lyric sheets! Imagine! People have quoted me whole verses of what they hear, as opposed to what's printed, sure that they are right and the cover (me) is wrong. Scary stuff, these egocentric individuals. I assure you, other than perhaps dropping an 'and' or a 'but', we take great care to make the lyric sheets accurate.[3]

Despite this response, the lyric has been corrected on later editions of the album.

The album features a photo, taken by Flip Schulke, of Galveston Seawall in Texas during Hurricane Carla of 1961. Syme layered other photos on top of this, including a photo of himself waving, Canadian model Paula Turnbull, and, most controversially, a newspaper with the headline 'Dewey Defeats Truman', referencing the famously incorrect headline that the *Chicago Tribune* published in reference to the 1948 US presidential election. Even thirty-two years later, the newspaper was still sensitive to its mistake and complained to the band. Syme subsequently changed the paper on the cover to read 'Dewei Defeats Truman'. On further releases, the paper's headline has been removed all together.

Another change to the cover is the removal, after a complaint by the company, of the Coca-Cola logo from the small billboards in the background. The logos have been replaced by the band members' surnames in similar typeface.

Moving Pictures

Release date: 12 February 1981
Current edition: Virgin/EMI CD
Recorded at Le Studio, Morin Heights, Quebec
Additional musicians: Hugh Syme—piano on 'Witch Hunt'
Produced by Rush and Terry Brown, Engineered by Paul Northfield
Engineer (Mixing): Terry Brown
Chart position: Canada: 1
UK: 3
US: 3

Rush's punishing routine of touring and writing meant that work on *Moving Pictures* had already begun in earnest during the *Permanent Waves* tour. Embryonic versions of 'Tom Sawyer' were performed ahead of recording while 'YYZ' was developed during several of the band's sound-checks. The result of this diligent work ethic was that *Moving Pictures* was released only a little over a year after its predecessor.

Many of the songwriting styles that the band had experimented with on *Permanent Waves* were fully developed and used to a much greater effect on this album, most notably (and appropriately, given the album's title) the decision to create imagery and narrative through the extensive use of programme-music.

Always keen to be at the cutting edge of technology, *Moving Pictures* was finished behind schedule owing to problems with Le Studio's digital mastering machine. The use of digital technology in the album's recording is responsible for its impressively crisp production, though some fans criticised the sound of the album as sterile—a criticism that would continue to be levelled at the band with increasing vigour for the coming decade.

Moving Pictures was an enormous success for the band, commercially and creatively. It was the band's highest selling album in the USA and is still the band's biggest selling album at the time of writing.

The band had finally applied the lessons they had learnt through years of writing, recording, and touring together and managed to distil Rush to its essence. Peart, who is sometimes disparaging of Rush's earlier work, has stated that it is with the release of *Moving Pictures* that the band really came of age. Once asked about the band's earlier albums, he replied: 'I really wish they would just go away. I think we really started ... wow, given my druthers, I would make our first album *Moving Pictures*. I can't think of a single reason not to do that!'[1]

Songs

'Tom Sawyer'

Opening the album with the now famous growl of Lee's Oberheim OB-X synthesizer, this unusual track was well-received commercially and with fans, being played on every Rush tour since its release.

The song's lyric began life as a poem by Pye Dubois, a friend of the band who was also the lyricist for the band Max Webster. Dubois' poem 'Louis the Lawyer' (sometimes referred to as 'Louis the Warrior') described a self-assured individual confidently making his way through the world. Peart modified and added to the poem, including 'the themes of reconciling the boy and man in myself, and the difference between what people are and what others perceive them to be'. The song's title references Mark Twain's famous character, whose rebellious independence and sceptical outlook ties in well to the subject of the song.

'Tom Sawyer' was performed live before its commitment to tape and early live recordings of the song show a marked difference; it is significantly faster than the final version. The decision to slow the song's tempo aids the connection between music and lyric with the steady pace bringing to mind the 'mean, mean stride' of the song's subject.

Although the song marks the beginning of a new era for Rush, the song features, in typical Rush fashion, a complicated instrumental section in an unconventional time signature. The instrumental section had its genesis in a riff that Lee would use to test his synthesizers during the band's sound checks. This riff was developed into a full part by the band before Lifeson completed the section with a fiery guitar solo. Lifeson used a cut-and-paste technique with his soloing, which he would go on to use with great effect when creating his solos on future albums:

> I winged it. Honest! I came in, did five takes, then went off and had a cigarette. I'm at my best for the first two takes; after that, I overthink everything and I lose the spark. Actually, the solo you hear is composed together from various takes.[2]

'Red Barchetta'

In 1973, a short story titled *A Nice Morning Drive* was published in *Road and Track* magazine. A keen car enthusiast, Peart read the story and based this song on it.

The story itself is a cautionary tale against the over-regulation and over-sanitisation of motoring that the story's author, Richard Foster, feared was not only removing pleasure from motoring, but also damaging drivers' sense of personal responsibility. Peart's lyric is a succinct and neat retelling of the story, which begins by describing a secret country place where the protagonist's uncle keeps a, now outlawed, Ferrari Barchetta in pristine condition. Enjoying his Sunday drive, the Barchetta is confronted by two 'gleaming alloy air cars', which, twice the width of the small sports car, spell disaster. With skilful driving, the protagonist races away and leaves the modern hulks stranded at a one-lane bridge, returning to his uncle's country hideaway.

The lyric and story have two major differences. Firstly, in Foster's story the two modern vehicles destroy each other in a head-on collision, while the wrecked sports car ends up damaged in a tree. Secondly, and most notably, the car types are entirely different. Peart's Ferrari replaces Foster's choice of an MGB Roadster.

From the mysterious opening and unveiling of the pristine car to the twists and turns of the thrilling chase, every part of the lyric is expressed musically. The song's mesmeric introduction fades in with Lifeson's memorable harmonic riff, while Lee's soft keyboards and Peart's cymbals underpin it. Lee uses the spacious arrangement to perform an introductory melody with his unmistakable overdriven Rickenbacker tone, something that particularly colours this song in comparison to many of the other tracks on *Moving Pictures*, where he opts for his newly purchased Fender Jazz bass.

While the song is a showcase for the proficiency of the band as songwriters and musicians, there is one notable mistake on the song—the word 'Barchetta' is properly pronounced 'Bar-ketta', something that was apparently pointed out to Lee by an Italian friend.

'YYZ'

The change to Rush's song-writing style is encapsulated neatly in this, the second of Rush's standalone instrumentals. Like its counterpart, 'La Villa Strangiato', the only other Rush instrumental to have been recorded by this time, it is an exercise in technical prowess for the three members of Rush. 'YYZ' features moments of thrilling musicianship throughout.

The instrumental, like 'La Villa Strangiato', shifts through numerous themes and styles, but, following the trend of other Rush songs of this era, it is considerably more concise, running to just four minutes and twenty-four seconds, less than half the length of 'La Villa Strangiato'.

Unusually, the writing process for 'YYZ' began in the air. One of the band's friends was an amateur pilot and offered to take the three of them on a pleasure flight over Toronto. Listening to the cockpit radio, the band heard the airport identification code for Toronto Pearson International Airport on their headphones. This code, YYZ, was represented audibly through Morse code, and is, in fact, the exact rhythm the listener hears repeated at the beginning of the track.

The piece successfully incorporates all three parts of the album's triple entendre artwork by being at once cinematic, emotive, and representative of travel.

'Limelight'

There can be few, if any, better examples of Rush's ability to incorporate complex and unusual time signatures into an apparently simple rock song than 'Limelight'. With a lyric that deals with the differences between seeming and being, this is particularly appropriate. It is clear from a first listen that 'Limelight' is a well-constructed song, but it is only upon delving into its composition that its complexity can be understood. This is all the more impressive given that the song itself runs at a relatively short four minutes and nineteen seconds, and that it has a fairly standard song structure. It is this façade of simplicity that adds an even greater weight to the lyric.

The lyric is often cited as an exposition of Peart's difficulty in adapting to some of the unwelcome attention that comes with the great success Rush were beginning to enjoy at this time. The line 'I can't pretend a stranger is a long-awaited friend' is often quoted. While this meaning is clearly apparent, there are layers to this song that are more universal, and perhaps the 'underlying theme' is something more fundamental.

While Peart's experience of fame clearly had an impact on the thematic content of the song, the second half of the lyric relates to human interaction in a more general way, continuing with the themes that were discussed in 'Entre Nous'. The latter part of the lyric suggests (by quoting Shakespeare) that we are all performers, and that it is only by abandoning some of our vanity and pretence that we can get on with 'the real relation'.

The song describes fame as a universal dream, but perhaps the ultimate meaning of the song is that, like many ubiquitous dreams, it is a hollow one, and that fame is an unfortunate by-product of success, and not an end in itself.

Lifeson's solo on 'Limelight' is regarded as one of his best by fans, and Lifeson himself:

> I've always enjoyed the elasticity of that solo, particularly the way it sounds on the record. It has a certain tonality I just love. I do like playing the solo live, but I think I prefer listening to it on the album. On record, it has a magical quality to it—it really conveys the pathos of the song and the lyrics. I've never been able to re-create that live. I get pretty close, but it's never exactly the way it is on record. I'll keep trying, though.[3]

'The Camera Eye'

Taking its title from a section of John Dos Passos's *U.S.A.* trilogy, 'The Camera Eye', at nearly eleven minutes long, is an anomaly in an album that otherwise is notable for its concise songs. Interestingly, while many other, longer Rush songs feature a variety of themes, 'The Camera Eye' is essentially the same piece of music played twice with a similarly themed instrumental punctuating the final verse. That said, it is a brilliantly evocative piece of music that fits the theme of the album well, painting a vivid picture of two of the world's great cities: New York and London.

Peart had by this point in his life visited New York numerous times as well as living in London as an aspiring musician. His passion for travel would, years later, align with his abilities as an author when he published several travel memoirs. The vibrant images portrayed by this song's lyric show many of the hallmarks of his later travelogues: a clear focus on the history and make-up of the locations, as well as considerations for the winners and losers of the society—'The focus is sharp in the city'.

The song's lengthy introduction with its suspense-building synthesizer and martial drumming is a rare example of Rush using a single simple theme for a large section of the song. The song's powerful chords and synthesizer-driven sound give it an unusual timbre—as if Emerson, Lake and Palmer were performing The Who's 'Baba O'Reilly'. There are no unexpected changes or musical breakdowns: it is simple, strident, powerful music. The bustling of the city, car horns, whistling of traffic wardens, and the impatient calls of citizens all help to create yet another moving picture in the mind of the listener.

The first verse focuses its attention on New York, while the second is about London. Musically, each verse is nearly identical, while the lyrics, in considering the cities' similarities, arguably suffer the same repetitiousness.

The song's instrumental section, towards the end of the song, is a blast of power with a thrilling high-paced Lifeson solo, powerful hard rock drumming from Peart, coupled with the attacking gravelly clang of Lee's Fender Jazz bass.

As the song fades out, the unmistakable bong of Big Ben can be heard; one of two samples used for the London section of the song. The other, which occurs eight minutes and fifty-four seconds into the track, is a mystery voice loudly burping before yelling 'mornin' guv'.

'Witch Hunt'

Subtitled 'Part III of Fear', this was in fact the first part of the 'Fear' series to be composed. Peart decided to write the series of songs after speaking to a friend who believed that—contrary to the belief of many—man's fundamental drive did not come from positive emotions such as love or reason, but from fear. Peart, interested by this idea, decided to explore different types of fear through a series of lyrics.

'Witch Hunt' deals with man's most primitive fear—the fear of 'the other'—and how this can feed a mob mentality. The carefully written lyric is aimed potently at those who would criticise anyone for what they are, rather than what they do. The entire lyric is written with a sharp precision, and one of the most effective lines of the song shows the utter absurdity in limiting freedom of expression: 'Those who know what's best for us/Must rise and save us from ourselves'.

The dark images conjured by the lyric are accompanied by an impressively brooding musical score. The ranting of a furious mob can be heard at the beginning of the track while ominous keyboards (incidentally another guest performance by Hugh Syme) gradually fade in. The doom-laden sound is completed by the tolling of a tubular bell.

Driven by Lifeson's stormy guitar, this song is another departure for Rush; there are no fast runs or explosive solos—the excitement of 'Witch Hunt' comes from its layers of textures and an almost perfect link between music and lyric.

While the song itself is anything but humorous, the studio technique used to produce the effect of the angry mob in the song's introduction has an amusing story behind it. Alex Lifeson recalled:

> We went outside of Le Studio and it was so cold, it was really cold; we were well into December by then, I think. We were all out there. We put a couple of mics outside. We started ranting and raving. We did a couple of tracks of that. I think we had a bottle of Scotch or something with us to keep us warm. So as the contents of the bottle became less and less, the ranting and raving took on a different flavour. We were in the control room after we had laid down about twelve tracks of mob—in hysterics.[4]

'Vital Signs'

Opening with a persistent sequencer sample, this reggae-flavoured piece is a taste of what is to come on the band's next album, *Signals*. Heavily influenced by The Police, this song's deliberately thin arrangement is a world away from the powerful proto-metal that Rush were so well known for only a few years prior.

The lyric to 'Vital Signs' is another of Peart's powerful calls to action, encouraging persistence in difficult circumstances. The lyric compares humanity and our daily actions and interactions to those of the machines we have created. Using the 'techno-speak' of the emerging digital world to represent these fundamental parts of humanity, it is an unusual lyric, but one that rewards multiple listens.

The song was composed, according to a hyperbolic Geddy Lee, 'in about five minutes' at Le Studio. This perhaps explains the immediacy of the piece. While the structure of the song is fairly traditional, the rhythmic approach is unprecedented in a Rush song. Perhaps because of this, fans were initially unconvinced by the song when it was performed live. The band, excited by their new direction and determined for the song to receive the recognition it deserved, decided that instead of dropping the song, they would in fact put it in the most exciting part of the set and begin their encore with it. It is now looked upon as a vital part of the Rush catalogue; the song pinpoints a moment of transition for the band that would impact their career forever.

Interesting Liner Notes

Aside from the famous triple meaning of *Moving Pictures* being expressed visually on the front and rear of the album's inlay, opening the booklet reveals a photograph of each of the band members. Each of these photographs is a layering of multiple exposures, thus creating a picture of movement—yet another expression of a moving picture.

The liner notes themselves reveal Peart's growing list of percussion, including, simply, 'plywood', which is used to create the unusual cracking sound in 'YYZ'.

Thanks are extended in the form of a lengthy list of 'Fabulous Persons'. The typically unusual list includes 'Max Lobsters', 'Loveman, Lovewoman & The Lovemachine', '*Asteroids*', and '*Volleyball*'.

'The Dept. of Above-And-Beyond' list thanks their long-serving producer Terry Brown, or—as is written in the liner notes—'Dear Olde Broon'. Unbeknownst to Brown at the time, this would be the penultimate studio album he would produce for the band, and surely the zenith of his career as a producer.

9

Signals

Release date: 9 September 1982
Current edition: Virgin/EMI CD
Recorded at Le Studio, Morin Heights, Quebec
Additional musicians: Ben Mink—electric violins on 'Losing It'
Produced by Rush and Terry Brown, Engineered by Terry Brown and Robbie Whelan
Chart positions: Canada: 1
UK: 3
US: 10

After the success of *Moving Pictures*, it became clear to Rush that the years of critical dismissal and commercial uncertainty were, at least in the main, behind them. After finding the enormous success that had eluded them for so long, it must have been a tempting prospect to go back into the studio to produce a formulaic clone of the album that had done so much for the band commercially. Thankfully, Rush continued to progress and produced yet another album of challenging new music.

Signals fully explores many of the ideas that were hinted at on *Moving Pictures*' final track, 'Vital Signs'. The album's instrumentation is largely driven by Lee's synthesizers, while the music itself is closer to contemporary pop than any preceding Rush album. Clear influences from art-rock bands such as U.K., Talking Heads, and, most clearly, The Police colour the album with a smattering of reggae and ska infusions.

Lifeson's guitar takes a far more textural role on *Signals*, with its normal position in the mix now often occupied by Lee's keyboards. Each song (with the exception of 'Losing It') was designed with the intention of live performance, and thus, with Lee's increasing use of keyboards, his bass is notably absent for long periods of time on the album. However, with Lifeson's new position, Lee's bass, when played, is perhaps more dominant than ever, taking the part of a rhythm and occasionally lead guitar. As a consequence of these dramatic changes to the band's sound, many fans took an immediate dislike to the new album. Fans of Lifeson's guitar were disappointed with its reduced presence, while fans of Lee's bass were disappointed with the growing use of keyboards. Lee's abilities as a keyboard player rarely enthused many, and so the album is often particularly disregarded by musician fans of the band. However, the clever arrangements and fantastically composed pieces are a true progression in the band's song writing, and their lack of ego in their decision to serve the song above all makes *Signals* one of Rush's greatest successes artistically, if not commercially.

Signals was the first album of Rush's controversial 'keyboard' era and was critically slammed primarily for this reason. Fans had mixed responses, many feeling it was a betrayal of their progressive routes, while others appreciated the exciting new direction of the music. The album sold well in Canada, immediately reaching number one on the album charts, but international sales were more modest.

At once a new beginning and an end, *Signals* is notable for its movement of Rush into a more contemporary sound, but it was this decision by the band that ultimately ended their relationship with their long-term producer Terry Brown.

Time has been kind to *Signals* and it has retrospectively been praised for its excellent composition, interesting arrangements and the tasteful but impressive musical proficiency displayed by the band throughout the album. 'Subdivisions' has become an anthem for many Rush fans and it has been regularly performed live since the album's release.

'Subdivisions'

Starting as they mean to go on with Lee's lone synthesizers, this is Rush truly adopting the new musical technology, and style, of the early '80s. The band produces an evenly paced and relentless industrial beat, bringing to mind the uninspiring uniformity of the suburbs the lyrics later describe. Peart's occasional blast of furious drumming, played against the steady stride of Lee and Lifeson, give a sense of the desperation to escape from the uninspiring sterility that these environments seem to impose on so many adolescents.

The lyric is a cyclical one that describes the eternal societal pressure to conform, and particularly the suffocating sterility of suburban housing subdivisions. The suburbs are described as a lonely place for 'the misfit' and 'the dreamer', and the song goes on to describe youthful alienation with the famous line: 'Be cool or be cast out'.

'Subdivisions' also features a rare vocal performance by Neil Peart. It is his voice that can be heard speaking the song's title during the pre-chorus section.

While the song is clearly a tonic for the aforementioned dreamers and misfits who so often relate to it, it is also a warning. The second verse of the song, which is frequently overlooked, describes the result of living with enormous pressure on one's dreams. The frustrated hopefuls are described as losing 'the race to rats' and being 'caught in ticking traps'. With their dreams now abandoned, the crushed misfits return to where they started and begin the sorry tale again back in the suburbs.

As on *Moving Pictures*, the opening track is synthesizer heavy and features instrumentation designed to serve the song as a whole. Much of the technicality that some Rush fans had grown to love is not present here. The heavy rock feel that still somewhat existed on the band's previous album is also heavily diluted by synthesizers, but this was a deliberate move by the band. Many fans considered this new direction something of a betrayal and were extremely disappointed by Lifeson's light rhythm guitar that, in many cases, took on a background role to Lee's keyboards.

Despite its initial frosty reception by some fans, the single performed well, charting at No. 8 in the USA. The song also marks a turning point for Peart's lyric writing, which would affect his writing for the rest of his career: '"Subdivisions" happened to be an anthem for a lot of people who grew up under those circumstances, and from then on, I realized what I most wanted to put in a song was human experience.'[1]

'The Analog Kid'

In many ways a companion piece to 'Subdivisions', this song relates to many of the same themes, but has a contrasting positive and exuberant outlook, which is also expressed through the music. While 'Subdivisions' described a longing to escape, 'The Analog Kid' is a song about the need to explore. An important distinction.

The entire song is sung from the point of view of a boy on the cusp of manhood and describes, at a great pace, thoughts running through his mind. The lyric is skilful in using very few words to describe a rich scene of an idyllic childhood memory.

The song opens with a speedy riff with the guitar and bass in unison, somewhat similar to the technical sound that was prevalent in Rush's early days, but distinctly coloured by the softer sound that Rush had now opted for.

The song progresses at a rapid pace, and the bridge section of the song includes several lines that perfectly describe the restless youthful confusion for which endeavour is the only cure: 'Too many hands on my time/Too many feelings—/Too many things on my mind/When I leave I don't know/What I'm hoping to find/When I leave I don't know/What I'm leaving behind'.

This section is followed by what is surely Lifeson's most thrilling moment on the album, and arguably one of his greatest ever recorded: the frenetic and hyperactive guitar solo that so perfectly encapsulates the song's lyric. Similar in some respects to the avant-garde solo he performs on 'Natural Science', this is a solo that one may say only Lifeson could perform. It is full of fast and lengthy runs, but is at once jazzy and lyrical.

'The Analog Kid' is an excellent example of Rush's keenness at this time to match the music with the lyric. The exciting and restless music, coupled with the dreams of youth, make a perfect match.

'Chemistry'

The last Rush song that would feature a lyrical contribution from Lee or Lifeson, this piece is unique in that the lyric was, in fact, a collaboration by all three members of the band. Consequently, the lyric itself has a style all of its own. Peart's intelligent and concise metaphor coupled with a vibrant and eminently sing-able choice of language make this a pleasing lyric. Less precise than many of Peart's individual efforts, but considerably less esoteric than Peart's collaborations with Pye Dubois.

The music shows a huge influence from The Police with its ska groove and highly syncopated drums, but also breaks new ground for Rush with its coupling of synthesizer and guitar to create harmonies. The great influence on Alex Lifeson of the guitarist Allan Holdsworth is also apparent on this track, most notably on the fast and complicated repeating patterns but also on the playful and improvisational guitar solo that is performed at the end of the song.

This song, remarking on the mysterious scientific truth behind matters of the heart invites a discussion of the scientific and physical background of what appear to be abstract things: music, emotion, and human interaction. It is appropriate that this brilliantly succinct song, about mysterious connections, shows the skill of Lee, Lifeson, and Peart, not just as the skilful individual musicians that they undoubtedly are, but as collaborators keen to serve the song above all.

'Digital Man'

A companion piece to 'The Analog Kid', 'Digital Man' further considers the subjects of the album's first two tracks. While 'The Analog Kid' describes a free and unrestrained character, 'Digital Man' describes a rigid and regimented man who compartmentalises and manages his life in a computational fashion, rushing through life without rest, despite his 'Date with fate in a black sedan'.

In the same way that 'Subdivisions' describes the dreams of youth being abandoned in favour of the rat race, 'Digital Man' is perhaps a development of this idea. A warning to any 'analogue kids' that might be giving consideration to abandoning their dreams in favour of the regimented and sterile life that it sometimes feels like society demands of us.

While this interpretation of the song is valid, it is worth mentioning that the certain advantages that digital technology has over analogue were not lost on the band who, as time progressed, became ever more digitised. Perhaps, in a way, harking back to *Hemispheres*, these two songs demonstrate the importance of balance. After all, dreams need determination and drive to be brought into reality while living life as a headstrong worker without rest or relaxation is equally damaging.

The band, in their quest to continue to progress their sound, mixed numerous disparate styles into this song. With its incorporation of reggae, ska, synth-pop, and rock, the band had achieved a new milestone in their songwriting and were very pleased with the piece. Producer Terry Brown, however, was not. This led to friction within the studio, and it has been said that the disagreement over this song—one that is central to the album—was partially responsible for the decision to produce the next album without him.

As well as its mixture of styles, this song is notable for its deft and agile rhythm part. Some of Lee's most adventurous bass playing can be heard throughout the song, while Peart's ability to mould his drumming around the song's unusual stylistic choices is impressive. Lifeson's jangly guitar and colourful chord usage is typical of the album and the unexpected bluesy solo is yet another hidden gem in this fantastically complex pop song.

'The Weapon'

Beginning life as one of Lee's synthesized sonic experiments, 'The Weapon' is yet another stylistic departure for Rush, at times approaching the territory of electronic dance music. This song, the second part of the 'Fear' series, describes the terror of the tyrannical. Initially bringing to mind the government of a superpower in the song's first line, Franklin D. Roosevelt's famous statement has its meaning entirely changed by a question mark: 'We've got nothing to fear—but fear itself?'

Describing the power of governments and ideologies to exploit the fear of their followers, 'The Weapon' is a song on a grand scale thematically and is also the longest song on the album.

The first verse speaks of the tyranny of governments, while the second alludes to the danger of unquestioned religion. The former is described as an 'iron fist in a velvet glove' and the latter as 'a steely blade in a silken sheath'. Despite this brutal imagery and a song that's content is almost entirely on the subject of why these ideologies ought to be feared, an incisive final line reveals a universal truth about all tyrannies: 'The knowledge that they fear/Is a weapon to be used against them'.

While the song is notable for being one of the most electronic that Rush would ever produce, the sparse and ambient instrumental section gives space for one of the most lyrical guitar solos that Lifeson would ever put on record.

'New World Man'

With its working title 'Operation 3:42', the genesis of 'New World Man' began towards the end of the *Signals* sessions. Producer Brown suggested the band write a short song to even out the sides of the album's length and fill the remaining three minutes and forty-two seconds available to them on the cassette tape format.

The song was composed in a single day and recorded fully the next, meaning the band had little time to adorn it with the usual rhythmic flourishes and complexities. Consequently, the song is simple with an easy and spacious feel. Despite the fact that the song was something of an afterthought for the album, it is the only Rush song to ever chart the American Top 40 and was No. 1 in the Canadian national singles chart.

Like 'Vital Signs' on the band's previous album, 'New World Man' begins with a repeating sequencer pattern before the band join in with a reggae groove. A powerful rock hook makes the song's chorus a memorable moment of the album and the playful feel that colours the whole song is a cheerful contrast to the album's previous track.

The lyrical content of the song appears to be on a similar theme to 'Beneath, Between and Behind' from 1975's *Fly by Night* album. While seven years prior Peart had been highly critical of the apparent failure of the American dream, 'New World Man' seems a more hopeful and considered case for the USA. Considering problems such as pollution and gun control, the song is neither a blatant criticism nor a platitudinous love song—it is the song of an observer, and one that has clearly been well considered.

Fading out at the last available second, 'New World Man' was one of the happy accidents that made *Signals* a brilliant album. With its simple structure and interweaving melodies it is surely a highlight of the album.

'Losing It'

This haunting piece features another of Rush's rare collaborations with an outside musician. Performed by Ben Mink, well known for his collaborations with K. D. Lang, and at the time performing in the band FM, an extensive electric violin part was added to the song. In addition to the textural melody added underneath the main body of the song, there is also an aggressive jazz-fusion-inspired violin solo that adds to the unexpected and unusual nature of the song. Despite this, 'Losing It' is by no means a gimmick and the violin was clearly written as a central component of the piece rather than being added as an afterthought.

Despite the totalitarian themes of 'The Weapon', the lyrics to 'Losing It' are, in tone at least, the darkest on the album. The lyric at first refers to an unknown dancer who, desperately nostalgic for her former glory, is now old and infirm: 'She limps across the floor/And closes her bedroom door'. The second verse alludes to Ernest Hemingway who, after enjoying immense success as a writer throughout his life, eventually found his body and mind collapsing under the strain of mental and physical ailments. The author, whose works *The Sun Also Rises* and *For Whom the Bell Tolls* are referenced in the lyric, eventually committed suicide after losing much of his sight and ability to write. It is regarding this tragic loss of ability, and others like it, that Peart penned the mournful line: 'Sadder still to watch it die/Than never to have known it'.

Peart's lyrics, even those that have their basis in anger or fear, are so consistently forward looking that this gentle, yet hard-hitting song is immediately subcutaneous. It is easy to wonder if Peart considered his own future when working on this song. At the time of writing, he was at the height of his powers as a lyricist and a drummer, but all things end, and perhaps it is this dark undercurrent that makes this lyric so effective.

'Countdown'

In the liner notes to *Exit...Stage Left*, thanks were offered by the band to those at NASA who had invited Rush to be part of a select group to view the first launch of a space shuttle. The band, who were thrilled by the experience, decided soon after that they would endeavour to compose a piece about the launch.

Using many of the techniques that were used so effectively on *Moving Pictures*, this song is cinematic in sound and lyric. With its brooding, tense opening, along with the sound of patrol jets and helicopters, the stage is set for an incredible event. Although this is another track with very heavy synthesizer use, the prominent guitars, shifting time signatures, and linear song structure make this the closest Rush would come for a long time to returning to the progressive sound that had dominated their 1970s output.

The NASA radio samples are used to great effect throughout the song, adding further to the tension during the 'countdown' section of the song. As the rockets ignite, the music suddenly opens out and the tense suspense is immediately transformed into triumphant relief.

'Countdown' is unique for several reasons, though not least in that it includes the sole example of a synthesizer solo on a Rush album. While Lee had frequently used keyboards to perform melody parts or breaks—this is the only time Lee has ever broken into a fully-fledged solo.

Despite choosing this grand song to finish the album with, the band would later distance themselves from the piece with Lee once referring to it as 'a pretty poor song' (Lifeson, however, did claim to like the piece in the same interview). Like many Rush songs, however, it was an experiment and Peart was more pragmatic in his criticism: 'Countdown' is another example of a song that didn't work at the time but led us forward. It was our first attempt at a documentary, taking real life and putting it into a song.'[3]

Arguably any song that is journalistic of a historic moment is likely to become dated, and perhaps it is this that has earned 'Countdown' derision from its writers. However, the song neatly and thematically concludes a landmark album for Rush. As Houston's high-frequency radio transmissions fade away before the record ends, it is pleasing to compare them to the other 'signals' referenced on the album. Not least the chemical ones on the cover.

'Countdown' was appreciated by NASA as a tribute to the space shuttle programme, and was used as a wake-up song for the crew of *Columbia* on its last successful mission.

Interesting Liner Notes

As well as referring to Lee, Lifeson and Peart as Pitcher, First Base, and Third Base respectively, Terry Brown is referred to in his production credit as Left Field.

Continuing the theme of *Signals*, the band's portraits are given an effect of infra-red images, although the images do not appear to be genuine infra-red photos.

Thanks are given by way of a list of 'Most Valuable Persons' to many individuals, but notably to 'The Griffin family and the people of NASA'.

The 'Department of Public Works, TORONTO' are thanked for the use of their fire hydrant on the cover. The dog, however, is not obviously thanked.

The image on the rear of the inlay is an artificial blueprint of a housing subdivision and on it references are made to the band members' nicknames with the use of 'Olde Dirk Road', 'Lerxtwood Mall', and the company 'B. J. Pratt & Assoc.'

Grace Under Pressure

Release date: 12 April 1984
Current edition: Virgin/EMI CD
Recorded at Le Studio, Morin Heights, Quebec
Produced by Rush and Peter Henderson
Engineered by Peter Henderson assisted by Frank Opolko and Robert Di Gioia
Chart positions: Canada: 4
UK: 5
US: 10

In 1983, Rush faced the most major personnel change since the departure of original drummer, John Rutsey. Unsatisfied with the production on *Signals* and keen to work with yet more electronic technology, the band decided something had to change. Producer Terry Brown, who had been instrumental in the development of Rush's sound since 1974, was equally unhappy with the synthetic direction the new music was taking, and so the working relationship between Rush and Brown was dissolved.

Initially, the band agreed to produce the album with Steve Lillywhite, but Lillywhite backed out of the project shortly before the start of the sessions, causing the band considerable difficulty. Lillywhite explains:

> Oh God, Rush hate me … they hate me. They hate me! Because I said I'd produce them, then I didn't. The only time I've ever almost been threatened with having my legs broken in the music business … by their manager![1]

With a commitment to a new album looming and difficulty finding a suitable producer to work with, the band decided to produce the album themselves, with assistance from Peter Henderson who had formerly worked with Frank Zappa, Supertramp, and King Crimson. The name of the album reflects not just the lyrical content, but the somewhat self-imposed pressure the band found themselves under in their desire to consistently progress.

Grace Under Pressure received strong, though mixed, reactions from fans and critics. Many were pleased at the introduction of a more guitar heavy mix after Lifeson had taken a back seat on *Signals*, though, equally, many of Rush's original fans who were desperate for a hard rock album were disappointed as Rush delved further into the world of synthesizers and electronic music.

In the end, this was a vital album for Rush's development, being the first without Terry Brown who had until this point been considered the fourth member of the band and had produced every Rush album to date. It also provided the developmental groundwork for what many, including Geddy Lee, consider to be one of the very best Rush albums: *Power Windows*.

Songs

'Distant Early Warning'

A rumble of synthetic noise quickly gives way to electronic drums and a blatantly contemporary new wave sound. The significant number of fans that were critical of Signals unprecedented use of synthesizers had clearly been ignored – the synthesizers are more to the fore than ever.

Geddy's formerly aggressive bass sound is far more restrained, while the guitars – soaked in reverb and chorus punctuate the bleak dystopic atmosphere. Despite the extensive use of electronic percussion, the chorus of the song is arguably more upbeat than anything on Signals.

The *Distant Early Warning Line* was an array of radar stations in northern Canada designed to detect incoming Soviet nuclear bombers. At the time this lyric was written the Cold War was at its height and the fear and paranoia of the time is reflected throughout this song.

Within the first few lines Geddy sings of an "ill wind" bringing "heavy water" and "acid rain". The lyrical expression of atomic war hits hard. This is a song of high pressure times, though unlike many of Peart's previous lyrics the content is not abstract but all too real.

The lyric discusses the fear of a loss of connection in a fast-moving world both on a personal level—'It's so hard to stay together passing through revolving doors'—and geopolitical level—'Cruising under your radar watching from satellites'—a personal fear of losing a relationship, a political fear of nuclear annihilation.

By choosing to split with Brown and to ignore those fans alienated by the electronic direction of the music, the band really had something to prove with this album, perhaps more so than any since *2112*. This driving opener pulls no punches and asserts Rush's independence once again.

'Afterimage'

After the Cold War imagery of 'Distant Early Warning' subsides, we are presented with a different kind of pressure: that of bereavement and grief.

A lyric that is specific enough to have real depth but that is broad enough to have meaning to many is hard to achieve. 'This is something that just can't be understood', and yet this powerful lyric makes a mean attempt.

As if to drive the point even harder, despite the undeniable nature of 'Afterimage' as a powerful rock song, Geddy completely forgoes the bass guitar in favour of his keyboards. Lifeson's guitar has a huge amount of space here, both producing dreamy textures and arguably the heaviest playing since *Moving Pictures*. An electronic breakdown section towards the end of the song picks up from where *Signals*' 'The Weapon' left off, though now we are hearing a band fully at home with their electronic direction.

'Red Sector A'

The name of this song is completely ambiguous. It in fact comes from the name of the area from where the band watched *Columbia* launch in 1981: that site of such hope and optimism. This ambiguity, this meaningless clinical title, is part of the horror that this song about a nameless, timeless place evokes.

Geddy Lee's mother was interned in the Nazi concentration camp at Bergen-Belsen until it was liberated by the forces of the UK and Canada in 1945. She had remarked to her son, who then relayed on to Peart, that she simply could not believe there was any civilisation left:

> I once asked my mother her first thoughts upon being liberated. She didn't believe [liberation] was possible. She didn't believe that if there was a society outside the camp how they could allow this to exist, so she believed society was done in.[2]

The song asks the question 'are there any human beings to survive?' A simple question, with a complicated answer.

Anyone listening to this song would be likely to surmise it was recorded in the early '80s. The synthesizers are brash, and the song is more electronic than any other on the album; however, it remains a powerful song about a subject that is almost impossible to relate to without resorting to platitudes or cliché—neither of which are present here.

'The Enemy Within'

The ska and reggae stylings that were touched on occasionally on *Signals* are fully realised in this song, part one of the 'Fear' series. Whereas part two and three had dealt with fear caused by external threats, this song describes the unhelpful nature of self-induced fear: hyper-vigilance and paranoia.

A frantic bass line, punctuated by jagged chorus-laden guitar chords, soon gives way to a dreamy electronic post-chorus section. The frantic and ambiguous nature of the music suits the lyric, which arguably provides the first glimmer of optimism on the album.

The fearful verses give way to a defiant chorus: 'I'm not giving in to security under pressure/I'm not missing out on the promise of adventure/I'm not giving up on implausible dreams'—a motivation to defeat 'The Enemy Within'.

'The Body Electric'

The second half of the album begins with the ubiquitous synthetic drum sound of this era. Taking the modern listener immediately back to 1984, our auditory panorama is filled with a machinic, juddering drum beat that is soon joined by the twang of Geddy Lee's 'popped' bass intro. The intro gives way to the lush keyboard and guitar that we have by, this point, begun to expect from this album.

The lyric, on first listen, appears to be simple. An entertaining science-fiction story of a rogue android trying to break free of its programming and the code that imprisons it. As with most Rush lyrics, however, there are deeper and more satisfying ways to interpret it: 'It replays each of the days/A hundred years of routines/Bows its head and prays to the mother of all machines'. Machinelike, our daily routines continue on and on as we follow our programming. This song appears to be yet another call to arms for the individual to seek and fight for freedom, like this android protagonist.

Rush's interest in technology has been plain to see from the subjects of their songs and the technology used to produce them. It has been noted that the refrain of this song '1-0-0-1 0-0-1' is the binary for the letter 'I' in the ASCII computer language.

A frantic and thrilling instrumental section in the middle of the song proves to any doubters that Rush had not lost interest in their traditional Rock instruments. Alex Lifeson's guitar solo draws influences from the previous decade's funk guitarists before leading into a brilliantly colourful display of rock lead guitar. The bass and drums provide a thrilling backdrop to a guitar solo that surely restored the faith many had lost in Lifeson after the back seat he appeared to take on *Signals*.

'Kid Gloves'

It is in traditional Rush style that what is probably the most accessible track on the album is far more complex than it first appears. The song begins with an upbeat arpeggiated guitar riff, segues seamlessly into a catchy pop rock chorus, and returns back to the verse—all the while without announcing to the listener that the time signature has changed from 5/4 to 4/4 (common time) and back again. The fact that Rush are able to write such interesting and truly 'progressive' music and almost hide it in what appears to be a pop song speaks volumes for their exceptional and efficient writing style at this time in their career.

The lyric to 'Kid Gloves' is one of the more ambiguous on the album. It was written at a time when Peart's lyrical style was, for the first time, becoming less specific and more holistic in its approach. This lyric describes the challenges of growing up in an undiscovered world and the maturation process that we all go through to a lesser or greater degree. In the first verse, Peart writes that it is 'cool to be so tough'. In the second, the phrase is reversed: 'it's tough to be so cool'. A simple lyrical trick that works well.

After a crescendoing guitar solo and the reprise of the irrepressible chorus the song finishes with a series of grin-inducing false-finishes, which bring this deceptively clever song to an end.

'red lenses'

With the title and lyric uniquely printed all in lower case, it seems Rush were attempting to make clear that this song was an unusual one. By far the most esoteric lyric on the album, 'red lenses' is a jazz-infused stream of consciousness that paved the way for the sound Rush would later perfect with their next album.

With the bass and drums holding close to a rigid composition, this piece is clearly influenced by much of the contemporary electronic music of the era—particularly the bridge section that begins the second half of the song. This section, the style of which had been unprecedented in a Rush album, features an atmospheric synthesizer which underlies a Neil Peart solo of drums and tuned percussion.

The lyric, one of the most interesting and unusual aspects of the song, was discussed by Peart shortly after the album's release:

> I can take someone like T.S. Eliot, who has influenced me greatly over the last few years, and realize that what he was doing was just throwing so many images at you all the time that you were left dizzy. But at the same time you were left with something. You were stepping into another dimension. So I use that idea. On a song like 'red lenses' from the *Grace Under Pressure* album, I tried to construct a series of ongoing images that just came at you. The colour red was the theme of it, but I twisted it in so many ways. It was the hardest thing I ever wrote, because I was trying not to say anything, and each line was saying something but at the same time it was trying to be so obscure and so oblique about the way I went around saying it—on purpose. It seems confounding, but in the end you're left with something. T.S. Eliot's poetry is the same way to me. At the end of it I don't really know what I've read, but it comes back to me. When I think of The Lovesong of J. Alfred Prufrock or The Wasteland I can't quote lines from them, and I can't say I understand everything that was said, but they move me.[3]

This track is a strange, but vital Rush song that helped develop the band's songwriting, production style, and indeed much of Peart's future live drum solos.

'Between the Wheels'

After the anomalous surrealism of 'red lenses', the foreboding synthesizers at the beginning of 'Between the Wheels' give way to the formidable growl of Lifeson's down-tuned guitar and Peart's thunderous drumming. The darker sound of the beginning of the album is back, in a far more ominous way for this finale.

The song, with its multiple meanings, alludes once again to the Cold War, which seemed at the time to be immediately capable of turning hot at a moment's notice: 'You can fall from rocket's red glare/Down to brother can you spare?/Another war?/Another wasteland?'

The contrast between the 'Rocket's Red Glare' so famously and patriotically alluded to in the 'Star Spangled Banner' and the 'Rocket's Red Glare' that may spell nuclear annihilation ('another war—another wasteland') is almost brutal. This song is full of colourful metaphor and an analysis by anyone but the listener may spoil the pleasure of its discovery. It is worth mentioning that it was at around this time Peart began to spend more time 'Between the Wheels' himself, while cycling his pushbike on tour. A slow fade out draws the song to a close before whilst the band improvise over the doomy riff.

With this excellent final song—a live staple to the end of Rush's career—one of the toughest albums of Rush's career was finished.

Interesting Liner Notes

As well as the art by Hugh Syme, the inlay for *Grace Under Pressure* features a portrait by the famous portrait photographer Yousuf Karsh who had previously photographed legendary figures such as Martin Luther King, Winston Churchill, Albert Einstein, and Salvador Dali.

At the end of the list of 'Thanks' is this sentence, referring of course to their now ex-producer Terry Brown: '*et toujours notre bon vielle ami—Broon*' ('and always our good old friend—Broon').

11
Power Windows

Release date: 15 October 1985
Current edition: Virgin/EMI CD
Synthesizer Programming: Andy Richards and Jim Burgess
Additional Keyboards: Andy Richards
Strings Arranged and Conducted by Anne Dudley—recorded at Abbey Road Studios, London
Recorded at The Manor, Oxfordshire; Air Studios, Montserrat and Sarm East, London
Produced by Peter Collins and Rush
Engineered by Jimbo 'James' Barton
Choir arranged and conducted by Andrew Jackman
Chart positions: Canada: 5
UK: 9
US: 10

Although *Grace Under Pressure* had been an opportunity to continue with the new direction that Rush had been forging, the lack of a producer and the difficult preproduction process had meant the band had not been able to realise certain ambitions. Since their progressive-rock era in the late 1970s, Lee, Lifeson, and Peart had each been developing their own musical tastes: listening to contemporary pop, art rock, and reggae. A keenness to incorporate contemporary musical styles into the unique Rush sound was part of the reason for recruiting Peter Collins to produce their next album. Traditionally a pop producer, he had worked with artists as diverse as The Musical Youth and Tracy Ullman. Collins' work with British new-wave electronic artist Nik Kershaw showed his extensive knowledge of production techniques on modern electronic music and it would be this that would characterise the new Rush album with its tightly energetic shimmering production.

Recorded at The Manor and Sarm East in England, as well as Air Studios in Montserrat, this was the first time since recording *Hemispheres* that Rush would record outside their native Canada.

As well as using cutting edge technology in the studio, Rush would embrace another modern technology by making *Power Windows* the first Rush album to be released directly onto CD.

Songs

'The Big Money'

The album's opener begins with a blast of crisp guitars and bright synthesizers. A stark contrast to the dark timbre of *Grace Under Pressure*, the step up in production quality is immediately evident. Peter Collins was known by many in the recording industry as 'Mr Big' and this enormous, energetic, and well-separated production shows why. Just seconds after starting the album, it becomes clear to a listener that the band and their production team were making the most of the cutting edge recording technology of the mid-1980s.

Like 'The Camera Eye', 'The Big Money' is the second Rush song to take its title from a John Dos Passos work; this time from the third part of his *U.S.A.* trilogy. Like the novel, Peart's lyric is experimental in nature. The song's verses simply list the numerous and various ways in which big business and high finance are influenced by their pursuit of wealth, and indeed the way the abstract concept of wealth assumes an amorphous persona. Becoming an end in itself rather than a means—a master rather than a servant. Peart was deliberate in his attempt to temper his cynicism though:

> I didn't want the voice of the song to be totally in the voice of a cynical, anti-corporate reactionary, though, because things like the Ford Foundation do accomplish a lot of good. I mean, the church and worthy events like Live Aid are big money, too.[1]

While the song's timbre shows immediate similarities to the myriad of highly produced new wave and synth-pop that was extremely popular at the time, beneath the shimmering sheen of the song's production is Rush at their technical best. With typically complex drumming, an impressively mobile bass line and jagged slashing rhythm guitars, this is a unique blend of highly technical hard rock and 1980s pop, infused of course with an intelligent lyric. Lifeson's ordinarily histrionic and avant-garde guitar solo style is somewhat tamed in this song with a clearer focus on melody and fluidity.

This strong opener has a confidence that was somehow lacking on the band's previous effort. Positive and powerful, it seems the band are now demonstrating the best results of the previous album's experimentation.

'Grand Designs'

Opening with a repeating sequencer part, 'Grand Designs' is another heavily synthesized song but also, in Peart's highly syncopated drum part, features one of the last gasps of ska influence in Rush music.

Lee's vocal performance is especially impressive on 'Grand Designs', showing off his extensive vocal range along with his ability to perform the lyric in a meaningful way. It is a world away from the shrieks and wails he was famous for a decade before, but still retains the fiery enthusiasm that brought such energy to the Rush sound.

The lyric was written entirely separately from the music with a completed demo being given to Peart before a line of lyric had been written for the song.

Once again taking its title from a John Dos Passos novel, *The Grand Design*. This was Dos Passos's conservative critique of Franklin D. Roosevelt's New Deal and was highly critical of the enormous bureaucracy of big government. Peart's lyric describes frustration of a more personal kind.

Throughout all of Rush's music, there is a thread of individualism that is visible once again here: 'Against the run of the mill/Swimming against the stream'. While the song suggests the merit in retaining this individualistic streak, the final verse suggests that without challenging norms, progress is impossible: 'We break the surface tension/With our wild kinetic dreams'.

The plan for the end of the song had originally been a rapid fade out; however, while recording the song, Peart began punching-in over the repeating sequencer at the end of the track. Although this made the song longer than initially planned—and somewhat scuppered the plan of a traditional fade-out—Lee explains the reaction after hearing the playback: 'Everybody loved it, so we decided to keep it in.... Then we had to learn to play it onstage'.[2]

'Manhattan Project'

While each of the songs on the album relate to some aspect of power, this song, named after the secret American project to produce the nuclear bomb, is perhaps the one that discusses the most grave of all grand powers.

This song is an excellent example of the bold new decisions that Rush were making in terms of production and arrangement. In a remarkable move, this song features no bass or guitar during long sections of the song, and the arrangement is persistently sparse, which Lee commented on:

> We pulled things out, but tried never to lose the focus of the trio. In 'Manhattan Project' on verse one and verse three its vocals, drums, and keyboards. This is not a typical thing for this band. Let's pull the bass and guitar out? How can you do this to a Rush song? But it worked and I loved the effect of it.[3]

While Rush are paradoxically typified by their constant changes, one aspect of their sound that is consistent is their highly energetic explosive hard-rock. Despite the laid-back verses, 'Manhattan Project' has an enormous and fast-paced chorus, cinematically contrasting the technical theory of the bomb, discussed in the verses to the chorus's awesome and terrifying imagery of its practical application.

After the song's final verse, there is an atmospheric instrumental section. Surprisingly, though, the lead lines are played by neither Lee nor Lifeson, but a string section.

The lyric was famously well-researched, with Peart, long before the days of the internet, apparently reading a dozen books to ensure his facts were correct. Indeed, the succinct references are clear with each of the verses opening lines. In each verse, the listener is asked to 'Imagine'.

At first, 'a time ... in the dying days of a war'—the end of the Second World War. Secondly, 'a man ... 'A scientist pacing the floor/In each nation—always eager to explore'. While only one man is mentioned, Peart makes an often overlooked point that both Allied and Axis scientists were working towards the bomb, and indeed for many different reasons.

The third verse is more specific and asks the listener to 'Imagine a place' in 'the secrecy of the desert sand'. This refers to Los Alamos, a small town in New Mexico where the scientists working on the Manhattan Project were based. The final lines of the verse, 'All of the brightest boys/To play with the biggest toys/More than they bargained for', have dark multiple meanings. While the man known as 'the father of the atomic bomb', Robert J. Oppenheimer, felt terrible regret after the nuclear bombing of Japan, there were also instances of fatal radiation sickness by some scientists working on the Manhattan Project. This is demonstrated in an animation that Rush used to accompany the song during live performances. The fourth and final verse brings to mind another man. This time Paul Tibbets, the US Army pilot who flew the B-29 bomber *Enola Gay* on the mission to attack Hiroshima with a nuclear weapon.

It is remarkable that Peart was able to get so much information into a song that has fewer than 200 words. His extensive research was clearly worthwhile. The song is also particularly worthy of note as one of the few rock songs that discussed nuclear weapons without taking a political view. The song is deliberate in its impartiality and stands as a song about history, rather than another song in the catalogue of anti-nuclear protest songs. These protest movements are briefly alluded to in the song's chorus, suggesting that 'Fools tried to wish it away'.

There is only one point put forward within the song and it is one that is, realistically, unarguable. It is encapsulated in the song's final few lines: 'All the powers that be/And the course of history/Would be changed for evermore'.

'Marathon'

Lee's dextrous repeating bass line along with the steady pace of Peart's bass drum do a fine job of creating the image of a long distance runner's incessant strides. Lifeson's colourful chord voicings build and release tension, giving texture to this musical image.

'Marathon' was described by Peart as about 'the triumph of time and a kind of message to myself'.[4] The marathon that is mentioned in the song's title is, of course, a metaphor for life itself. A measured retort to the 'hope I die before I get old' and 'Live fast, die young' rock star clichés, 'Marathon' is a song that suggests it is possible to do the things that we want to do, if we are persistent and pace ourselves with intelligence: 'You can do a lot in a lifetime/If you don't burn out too fast'. A life well lived, according to this song, is a triumph of both sense and persistence.

With the line 'The heartbreak climb uphill', Peart is referring to the runner's term 'Heartbreak Hill'. This term is used to describe numerous difficult ascents during long-distance footraces. Whether it is nuclear weaponry or running, it is clear that care has been taken to research the lyrical subjects.

The song is another piece of Rush music that includes outside musicians. A transcendent musical lift is provided by a choir towards the end of the song. The string section that was recorded at Abbey Road studios also makes an appearance in 'Marathon'.

One of Ernest Hemingway's favourite mottos was 'First, one must last'. Peart paraphrased this simple line and included it as the final line of the song, which sums the piece up neatly: 'First you've got to last'.

'Territories'

While 'A Passage to Bangkok' included some moments of Eastern musical influence, they were short, stereotypical, and clichéd. 'Territories', however, was written after Peart had visited China and the influence of this post-revolution Communist nation on him can be heard in this song's lyric. The song's introduction brings to mind something of, at least, the Western idea of the Orient with its pentatonic scales and ambient, dreamlike quality. It is certainly a more mature effort in bringing this image to mind.

The main body of the song begins as a highly layered textural piece, highlighting Collins' mastery of the studio. This builds, gradually, into powerful funk-infused rock. The lyric is one of the angrier on the album and immediately demonstrates the absurdity of blind nationalism in its first line: 'I see the Middle Kingdom between Heaven and Earth'. Peart explains:

> As for the opening line about the Middle Kingdom—that's still what China calls itself today. The reason for the Middle Kingdom is because it's a middle between Heaven and Earth. In other words, it's slightly below Heaven—but still above everybody on Earth.[4]

The lyric is conversational, almost casual, in its tone and goes on to list example after example of the hypocrisy that exists in the mindset of the nationalist. However, despite China's inclusion early in the song, Peart is careful to mention that this is something that occurs 'in every place with a name'.

The second part of the song's chorus features another subtle lyric that is only revealed to those who read the lyric sheet. Criticising the insular and stagnant nature of some isolationists, it reads: 'In different circles/We keep holding our ground/Indifferent circles/We keep spinning round and round'.

The song's second verse discusses the pointlessness of certain kinds of patriotism. The ridiculous hypocrisy of emigrating to or invading another country, only to maintain one's patriotic fervour for the country of one's origin: 'Better people … better food … and better beer/Why move around the world when Eden was so near?'

The song's final section takes an immediate turn to a darker tone, and Lee's careful vocal performance reflects this. The brutal consequences of these ideas are suddenly sharp in focus as Lee sings: 'They shoot without shame/In the name of a piece of dirt'. The song is summed up finally by encouraging the pride in citizens of the world. At once independent and united. Undivided by flags or abstract notions of nation.

'Middletown Dreams'

Opening with a blast of power that gradually recedes, 'Middletown Dreams' paints an intimate picture of the imagined lives of a few individual men and woman that Peart saw while cycling through middle America when on tour. Dreams have been a regular subject of Rush songs since the band's beginning, and this is a somewhat ambiguous, but arguably optimistic, song about the importance of maintaining one's dreams—even if it takes time to realise them. Peart references real people who, despite their ordinary appearance, went out and achieved great things as authors, artists, and—somewhat autobiographically in the second verse—musicians. The character in the first verse is based on the author Sherwood Anderson who literally walked out of a small town and followed the railway to Chicago in order to begin his career as a writer. The painter in the final verse was based on Paul Gaugin, a French artist who left his job as a stockbroker in order to paint professionally.

The song's simple descriptions of its characters are not initially particularly complimentary, but give an impression of the depth that lies beneath the surface of quiet and apparently ordinary people. While the characters in the lyric make the decision to pursue their dreams, the song also describes the nourishing nature of as yet unfulfilled dreams: 'Dreams transport desires / Drive you when you're down'.

The song's passionate finale is an energetic bass solo from Lee. Full of the jazz-funk style that Lee was a proponent of at this time, the punchy nasal twang of his newly acquired Wal bass is particularly evident here.

'Emotion Detector'

With its heavy use of electronic drums, layers of keyboards, and sequencers, as well as guitars soaked in numerous digital effects, this is a song with a complex textural and instrumental arrangement. Owing to these factors and more, it was extremely difficult to record for the band.

'Marathon', with its string section, choir, and complex instrumental passage, caused some anxiety for the band, who were unsure if they could realise their ambition for the song in the studio, but they in fact found it remarkably easy to do so. 'Emotion Detector', for which there were no similar fears, was recorded with considerable difficulty.

As well as the concerns with meeting the demands of the song's technical and musical complexity, Peart was particularly concerned that the music for 'Emotion Detector' would properly complement his lyric. Owing to his dissatisfaction with Lifeson's guitar solo (which had been written and rehearsed for weeks in advance), the solo was rewritten and rerecorded in the studio.

The lyric was a candid exploration of human emotion by Peart, though it is far from a love song. Many of the song's lines seem to be a direct response, even an antidote, to the meaningless saccharine love songs that pervade so much popular music: 'Trust is just as rare as devotion/Forgive us our cynical thoughts'.

The song's chorus is an emotive lift both musically and lyrically and speaks of the shattered illusions that result from real honesty and intimacy. While these illusions are 'painfully shattered', it is at this point, finally, that 'discovery starts'.

Lifeson's razor sharp rhythm guitar cuts through the second verse where the song's incisive lyric continues to elucidate the truths that are so often ignored by pop music: 'It's true that love can change us/But never quite enough'. While we may fall in love, it seems that Peart is saying that we are never quite perfect partners for each other. It is, however, the hopeful chorus that serves as a salve to this tough point.

Arguably one of the best songs on *Power Windows*, and certainly one of the most complex, 'Emotion Detector' has never been performed live. Its unusual focus on emotion was an indication of Peart's future lyrical direction.

'Mystic Rhythms'

To conclude *Power Windows*, Rush attempt to describe the indescribable. The power of nature, the cosmos, and all that is beyond reason is brought to mind in this highly synthetic and almost ambient track.

Making extensive use of his versatile electronic percussion, Peart's drumming is the driving force throughout 'Mystic Rhythms', while Lifeson's acoustic guitars and Lee's swathes of keyboards add texture beneath Lee's vocal melody.

While many Rush fans now hold *Power Windows* to be one of their favourite Rush albums, this song is a perfect example of the enormous change that Rush made to their sound on this album. As Rush were now exploring songs that almost entirely departed from rock music, it is understandable that many of their former fans were unhappy with the band's direction. This piece was indeed such a change of tone for Rush that it was in fact featured as opening music for the

NBC's news programme *1986*. It is hard to imagine a television company using much of Rush's back catalogue for the same purpose. Regardless, those fans who enjoyed Rush's continual progression were thrilled with this unusual piece.

The lyric describes the fleeting moments of apparent realisation that occur to us when confronted with an amazing sight, sound, or moment: 'We sometimes catch a window/A glimpse of what's beyond'. Immediately, Peart, who appears to always have one foot firmly rooted in logic, asks: 'Was it just imagination/Stringing us along?' Although the true origin of these feelings of awe is unknown, Peart seems to be suggesting that the wonder is the reward.

With Lee's bass melody carrying the song through its final fade out, 'Mystic Rhythms' is an unusual but ultimately successful song that conjures awesome images and refers to impossibly complex thoughts and feelings in a recognisable way.

Interesting Liner Notes

Another excellent piece of work by Hugh Syme adorns the front of this Rush album and, once again on a Rush album, the title's multiple meanings are explored visually on the front and inside cover. The most obvious meaning of the term (the automotive one) is, however, not depicted anywhere in the album art.

While Jim Burgess had been previously credited as assisting with synthesizer programming, Andy Richards is now also credited as doing so, as well as playing additional keyboards.

Power Windows was recorded at a remarkably long list of locations. In addition to The Manor, Air Studios, and Sarm East, the string section was recorded at Abbey Road while the choir was recorded at Angel Studios in London.

Thanks are offered to (among others) 'Razor Willie, Fosforos Scoozball, the King of Antilles Television and HRH King Lerxst'.

'The ubiquitous B-man' was also thanked in the liner notes. This refers to Bill Banasiewicz who would later write the band's official biography.

This is the first Rush album to be 'Brought to you by the letter'; in this case, 'Brought to you by the letter M'. This refers, quite simply, to the number of tracks on the album that start with (or strongly feature) this letter.

12

Hold Your Fire

Released: 8 September 1987
Current edition: Virgin/EMI CD
Additional musicians: Andy Richards—keyboards
Aimee Mann—vocals
Synthesizer programming assistance: Andy Richards and Jim Burgess
Recorded at The Manor, Oxfordshire; Ridge Farm Studio, Surrey; Air Studios, Montserrat; McClear Place, Toronto and Lerxst Mobile
Produced by Rush and Peter Collins
Engineered by Jimbo 'James' Barton
Strings arranged and conducted by Steven Margoshes, recorded at McClear Place
Chart positions: Canada: 12
UK: 10
US: 13

Pleased with Peter Collins' work as producer on the preceding album, Rush recruited him once again to begin work on their twelfth studio album, *Hold Your Fire*.

The synthesizers and keyboards are still hugely prominent, and Lee, once again, works with Andy Richards who, as on *Power Windows*, performed some of the more technical keyboard parts.

The band returned to The Manor in Oxfordshire and AIR Studios in Montserrat to record, and they recorded additional material at Ridge Farm in Surrey and McClear place in their home city, Toronto. The numerous recording locations reflect the huge variety of sounds the band felt were required for the album. The various studios played host to strings, a brass band, a gospel choir, and an additional solo vocalist as well as Rush themselves.

While *Power Windows* was the first Rush album to be released directly to CD, *Hold Your Fire* was the first to take advantage of the longer running time now available to bands using this format. Consequently, with ten tracks and running to just over fifty minutes, *Hold Your Fire* was, on its release, Rush's longest studio album. This necessarily led the band to include material that would formerly have been cut from the final album and, arguably, reduces the overall quality of the finished product.

While the album would eventually attain 'Gold' status, sales for *Hold Your Fire* were initially modest. Peaking at No. 13 on the *Billboard* charts, it was the least successful Rush album since *Hemispheres*.

While *Hold Your Fire* generally features strong melodies and is arguably the finest voice Lee has ever been in, the pop-centred production and heavy use of synthesizers was another disappointment to those who craved another Rush rock record.

As well as the multiple meanings of the album's title, Peart has little to be criticised for in relation to this album; in fact, it is perhaps the most thematically strong of any Rush album to date, with each song having a close lyrical relationship to its predecessor.

Songs

'Force Ten'
The first song on *Hold Your Fire* is a song that almost did not make it onto the album at all—not owing to its quality, but owing to the fact that it almost was not written. During the last day of preproduction, Peter Collins suggested that the band write another song and, with Peart keen to use a newly finished lyric, Lee and Lifeson quickly composed 'Force Ten'.

The lyric was another collaboration between Peart and Pye Dubois, whose work had been the basis for 'Tom Sawyer'. As with their previous collaboration, Dubois initially sent Peart a poem that was then adapted and added to for the purposes of the lyric.

While Dubois' eccentricity is identifiable in the finished lyric, the song is clearer and more conventional than in his previous collaboration with the band.

The song takes its name from the Beaufort Wind Force Scale, which in fact rises to a stronger, but perhaps less aesthetically pleasing Force 12. The song alludes to persistent metaphorical storms that affect all of us. While it is somewhat ambiguous, the suggestion seems to be that one can respond to life's storms in numerous ways, but that rather than taking cover, one can 'ride the wind' and live life with a '*joie de vivre*'.

After the sampled pneumatic drill and laughter, Lee's bass provides the opening theme to the song. Inspired by his friend, fellow bassist Jeff Berlin, Lee makes the unusual decision to incorporate plenty of bass chords into his playing throughout the song. Now taking over the parts of bass guitar and rhythm guitar, with the now ubiquitous synthesizers, Lifeson's guitar is often relegated to the background. Nevertheless, 'Force Ten' is carried along by its driving rhythms and infectious melodies.

In 'Force Ten', Peart subtly pays homage to female Rush fans, of whom there appear to be a disproportionately small number in relation to their male counterparts. The line 'Cool and remote like dancing girls' was referred to by Peart in his book, *Roadshow*:

> I always loved to see females in the audience singing along, or air-drumming, or even dancing. However, given the complexity and constant changes in our music, even their dancing had to be absorbed in the music—no mindless twitching to a metronomic beat. In our song 'Force Ten,' I had expressed my appreciation for that absorption.[1]

'Time Stand Still'

Lifeson's metallic faux-acoustic guitar begins this song with his signature use of arpeggiated chords. An unusual blend of AOR, pop, and, as the subtle use of unusual time signatures from the outset reveals, progressive rock, 'Time Stand Still' was the lead single for the album.

Lyrically, a perfect continuation from the preceding track, the first lines 'I turn my back to the wind/To catch my breath' immediately bring to mind the violent and awesome storms that were mentioned in 'Force Ten'. Another subtle reference to the previous track is the line 'I let my skin get too thin', a stark contrast to the 'skin as thick as thieves' mentioned in 'Force Ten'.

The album's fast-paced opening stride gives way, with this second track, to a more considered, almost sombre tone. Lee sings Peart's lyrics with a convincing yearning, willing time to stop for a moment, long enough for some of life's better experiences to truly sink in and for the good times to last a little longer.

Rush once again collaborated with another musician on this track. Feeling the song could benefit from a female vocalist, they hired 'Til Tuesday bassist and singer Aimee Mann to sing part of the chorus and perform some of the song's backing vocals.

The endless ticking of a clock is brought to mind by Peart's percussion in the chorus. Wood blocks and high-pitched toms are carefully placed around the melody and add an additional unsung layer of meaning to the song.

While the song's emotional resonance is hard to fault, the music video has aged particularly poorly. Directed by experimental Polish director Zbigniew Rybczyński, the video's bizarre use of green screen to give the impression that the band were floating around a studio is a strange and unintentionally amusing image. Geddy Lee remarked on the video later on in the band's career:

> It's such a strange video. It was just a bizarre day.... This is my hair at its worst. It's a bad 'do. I don't even think we ever really nailed music videos. The funny thing is just watching this giant drum kit flying through the air. It's one thing to see humans. They have a form. But here's this whole drum kit floating through space. Who says we don't have a sense of humour?[2]

'Open Secrets'

With a similar arrangement to the album's previous two songs but perhaps lacking some of their melody and drive, 'Open Secrets' is a song that at first runs the risk of sounding formulaic. While Lifeson's light guitar was well suited to the album's previous two songs, its absence here is notable. The song's second half breaks down into a fusion of jazz and rock, which adds some additional colour to the song, but given the numerous musical tools at the band's disposal, it remains remarkably sonically static.

The song is perhaps an attempt to incorporate a large number of musical ideas that, in practice, are not ever fully developed. Rush have remarked that 'Open Secrets' took a great deal of time to compose.

While musically the song could be regarded as a weak point on the album, the lyric is yet another carefully composed piece by Peart. Inspired by a conversation he had with Geddy Lee, the words are another plea for honesty and openness within personal relationships. The song discusses the dilemma that faces us when we consider revealing tough truths—to unburden oneself and risk scorn, or to carry the weight, but with self-protection.

'Second Nature'

Lee's soft baritone atop a lush synthesized piano opens this song, which shows a maturation of Rush in numerous ways. While Rush in their early days were (often to their advantage) strongly opposed to compromise, 'Second Nature' is an 'open letter' that reveals an acceptance that one side of an argument will never win out completely, and that compromise is more acceptable than a complete abandonment of one's initial aim: 'I know perfect's not for real/I thought we might get closer/But I'm ready to make a deal'.

The double meaning of 'Second Nature' carries through the song, with a wish not just for the beauty of nature to carry through to our everyday habitats, but that it would seem, at least to the author, that this 'ought to be second nature' in itself. The song is something of a secular prayer, which opens as an open letter to basically anyone who will listen. Indeed, the line 'Now I lay me down in dreamland' was inspired by a prayer that Peart was taught as a child.

The rapidly moving melody lends itself to Collins' brittle production and the band's choice to arrange the song with hugely contrasting moments—from softly accompanied vocal to heavy drums and distorted guitar. The impressive musical use of light and shade successfully brings power to the song's most important moments.

'Prime Mover'

The philosopher, Aristotle, in his discussion of causes, found that the universe, unlike anything else, must have a 'Prime Mover', a force or being that is responsible for all of the movement within it. The term is also used in engineering to describe the part of a machine that converts energy into movement. These and the term's other meanings are thoroughly explored in this song, in sometimes subtle ways, that once again reveal Peart's avid consumption of literature.

The song's narrator takes an objective view of humanity and sees basic physical creatures responding to their instincts and, at first, simply surviving. As the song develops, so too do the creatures it describes: no longer responding simply to instincts, but now responding rationally to their passions. The meaning of their experiences, and their existence, becomes important to them.

Collins' pop-honed production brings Lee's vocal right to the fore on 'Prime Mover'. With its strong melodies and a meaningful performance of a complex lyric, it is a moment where it would seem that the music, lyric, and production are in perfect synergy.

Flashes of brilliant musicianship from the band decorate the track without becoming obtrusive and Peart's layered lyric continues to reward listeners time after time.

The final verse of the song refers overtly to Aristotle's use of the term with the lines 'I set the wheels in motion' and 'And run behind the scenes', which is an allusion to Aristotle's view that while a Prime Mover must exist, it is unlikely to have any concern for the results of its initial action. Led to its conclusion, this line of thinking leads to a realisation that (as pointed out in 'Freewill') destiny is not predetermined and, while certain things have been set in motion without our input, it is us that must decide how we respond to the world we find around us: 'Anything can happen'.

'Lock and Key'

One of the darkest tracks on the album, 'Lock and Key' deals with the brutal instincts that we carry, but hide behind a 'civilised veneer'. Like other tracks on the album, this piece is, at its core, about balance. This time, the balance between freedom and security. Accepting that while we carry this 'killer instinct', we must find a balance between silencing it entirely, and giving in to it.

The song's themes of imprisonment are given further depth by the inclusion of Peart's line 'The heart of a lonely hunter'. This is an allusion to Carson McCullers' debut novel about a deaf mute who suffers a further literal confinement in a mental asylum.

'Lock and Key' is a richly arranged piece with complex bass and keyboard lines occurring at the same time. Live, the melodies were amalgamated into one keyboard line giving the song a distinctly different sound. Musically, 'Lock and Key' is unique in Lee's use of a five-string bass.

The song's second verse with its unconventional African-inspired percussion, complex bass guitar sequences, and flashes of Andy Richards' synthesizers bring to mind the layered arrangements that were found on *Power Windows*. Despite the numerous complicated musical ideas, the music serves the lyrics well. This is partly due to the lyrics and music being written simultaneously.

The song's intensity reaches its climax with its finale—a short explosive drum solo in the song's final moments. Peart was particularly pleased with the results:

> That's fantastic, a beautiful exchange of roles: a drum solo in the terms of a guitar solo, where the rest of the band supports, Geddy and Alex playing the actual rhythmic pulse. It allows us to try out a new suit, to take on a new interrelationship between us.[3]

'Mission'

With the sound of a synthesized choir opening the song, it is abundantly clear that this song was produced in the late 1980s. While this type of production is often treated with contempt, and only openly appreciated with an expression of irony, the honesty of the lyrics on 'Mission' do something to make this track timeless. It is still, after all, extremely popular with Rush fans.

Despite the song's somewhat saccharine opening, the band blast into a powerful verse that is lifted further by Lifeson's carefully employed chords. Synthesizers dominate the song's body, but Lee's vocals once again carry the lyric with such sincerity that the song's nuts and bolts are easily ignored.

The song contains one of the most thrilling moments of music on the entire album with an unusual instrumental section full of time changes and bizarre musical flashes. Despite the poppy production, it is somewhat reminiscent of 'La Villa Strangiato' as Lifeson tortures his howling guitar before an entirely unexpected duet between Lee's bass and Peart's glockenspiel.

A similar song lyrically to 'Middletown Dreams', 'Mission' is a song that looks at the other side of dreams—not just the price of obsession, but also the struggle for those that are undecided or unsure of their own ambitions. The song grew from a conversation that Lee and Peart had about the idealised way people often viewed the life of a successful musician. The song explains that while realising one's ambition is of course an achievement to be proud of, every decision has its consequences and many of them are negative. While the majority of the song is sung from the point of view of someone whose wish is to obtain the drive and ambition of the people they admire, the final section of the song is a response to that feeling, and those that have it: 'It's cold comfort/To the ones without it/To know how they struggled—/How they suffered about it.../We each pay a fabulous price/For our visions of paradise'.

'Turn the Page'

Since recording the first Rush album, Lee's style of bass playing had evolved continuously. On 'Turn the Page', Lee uses an unusual style, plucking with both his thumb and fingers to employ something like a classical guitar finger-picking style. While Lee's bass playing had always been at the forefront of Rush's music, the simultaneous use of chords and root notes that open this song at once take the role of both rhythm and bass guitar.

Lee's ambitious bassline relentlessly drives the song, but caused him some trouble on tour. The vocal and bassline have little in common melodically or rhythmically, and consequently, he found it extremely difficult to perform both simultaneously when performing live. It is notable that twelve albums into their career, the band were still deliberately pushing themselves by writing music that was just beyond their technical reach.

With rapidly moving instrumentation, 'Turn the Page' makes fine work of representing the lyric. In it, Peart describes time as a river, carrying us at great speed into the future. Today is merely a time capsule, a moment that, before we realise it, will too be consigned to the past. 'Turn the Page' reminds the listener to engage with the present, and those who we find ourselves sharing it with.

Lifeson's powerful rhythm guitar makes a welcome return on this track and it is used to great effect in the bridge section halfway through the song. The musical breakdown that follows provides a stunning contrast when everything but Lee's bass is removed. Shortly after, Lifeson breaks into one of his eccentric signature solos. Using his personalised 'Lerxst Sportscaster' to bend notes from high wails to subterranean rumbles, it is a premonitory hint that Rush still maintain their rock roots.

'Tai Shan'

There are few Rush songs that inspire as much derision as 'Tai Shan'. Both Lifeson and Lee have distanced themselves from the piece with Lee describing it as 'an error'.[4]

The song takes its title from the easternmost of China's five great mountains. A place of worship and one of the most important ceremonial locations in China, Peart reached the summit in 1985 as part of an extended cycling tour of the country. Inspired by his experience, he wrote the lyric and was also involved in imbuing the piece with numerous authentic details. He based the drums around the woodblock rhythm that Buddhist monks use for their chants. The band also sampled a Shakuhachi flute, actually a Japanese instrument, but still an authentic sound of the ancient orient.

The piece is soft and atmospheric, similar in some ways to 'Mystic Rhythms', but the attempt to bring a Chinese sound to the song, coupled with its highly personal lyric, perhaps alienated some fans (and some of the band).

At the very end of the song, as it is fading out, careful listeners (or those who turn their volume up) can hear a reversed sample of Aimee Mann's voice from the 'Time Stand Still' sessions. Peart describes it as 'a nice texture which gave an eerie, pseudo-Chinese sound'.[5]

The line 'If you raise your hands to heaven/You will live a hundred years' is a reference to the legend that those who reach the mountain's summit will reach their century. Peart has only spoken positively of the song and its composition; if the legend is to be believed, though, there is plenty of time for him to change his mind.

'High Water'

Finishing the album off is another song that favours texture and atmosphere over the drive of hard rock. Recycling some of the ideas that were perhaps more fully realised on *Power Windows*, 'High Water' is something of an amalgamation of the Eastern rhythms of 'Territories' and the textural layers of 'Mystic Rhythms'.

In the lyric, Peart explores the numerous, and sometimes rarely considered, connections that mankind has to water. The fact that water literally flows through our veins and that without it our planet would be barren of life is quickly alluded to in the first few lines. The song goes on to consider water's power: to shape landscapes, to inspire longing, and relief. It is a lyric in which every line provides a new image, from the trickle of a mountain spring to 'torrents of tropical rain'.

Peart has mentioned that water, to him, has a therapeutic quality: 'I always feel comfortable when I'm near water, be it the sound of the ocean or even the refreshing feeling of a dip in the swimming pool'. And so yet another meaning is given then to the song's final line. The water takes me home.[6]

Interesting Liner Notes

In addition to the numerous musicians on the album, credit is also offered to The William Faery Engineering Brass Band who were recorded at Mirage Studio, Oldham.

Hugh Syme's Spartan front cover has some life breathed into it when opening the booklet wherein a revelatory and significantly more detailed picture is revealed.

Thanks are offered to, among others the Steve Morse Band and crew, Jeff 'Yankel' Berlin, Those Darn Fish, Patsy Cline, Luke Warm, and all cowboys everywhere.

Thanks are also offered to 'Rockin' F'. This is a fictional band created by the members of Rush to aid them in the writing process. It is basically shorthand for simple hard rock, and so, rather than going into a great detail about how to perform a part, one of Rush's members may just say 'Let's play this part like 'Rockin' F'.

The Gangster of Boats is also mentioned in the liner notes—Rush would go on to not write a trilogy of songs by this name.

Presto

Release date: 21 November 1989
Current edition: Virgin/EMI CD
Additional musicians: Rupert Hine—additional background vocals, additional keyboards
Jason Sniderman—additional keyboards
Recorded at Le Studio, Morin Heights, Quebec
Produced by Rupert Hine and Rush
Engineered by Stephen W. Tayler
Chart positions: Canada: 7
UK: 27
US: 16

As live album *Exit...Stage Left* had heralded the end of the prog-rock era for Rush, so the next live release, *A Show of Hands*, signalled the end of the band's synthesizer era. The band had become almost unrecognisable from the rock power-trio that had released their debut thirteen years prior. *Presto* was a deliberate reaction to this and an effort by the band to return to a simpler, more organic sound. Musically, the songs were considerably less layered with a focus on bass, drums, and guitar. Peart also took a new approach with his lyrics with a deliberate effort to make them less 'heavy'. He also took the decision to write about wide-ranging subjects rather than continuing his recent trend of following an individual lyrical theme throughout an album.

Although he would return as producer for 1993's *Counterparts*, Peter Collins declined to produce *Presto*. Consequently, the album was produced by Rupert Hine, the third Englishman to produce the band. As with each of the band's previous producers, Hine was encouraged to put his own stamp on the album. Although the album was notable for its back-to-basics approach (it features minimal keyboards in comparison to the band's other '80s efforts), the production is often regarded as sterile. This is a contentious point, however. Hine's production was a deliberate effort to create a powerful rock album that still maintained a good separation between instruments. It is almost impossible to argue that this was not achieved, and certainly audiophiles appreciate the dynamic range of the album. Those fans who were more used to the louder rock productions of the time remain disappointed with the album's sound, despite the more traditional approach.

Presto was an album of transition. Returning after the band's longest career break yet, working with a new producer, and going back to *Le Studio* for the first time since *Grace Under Pressure*, the album was always going to be different. With the band's decision to make the dramatic shift away from synthesizers, *Presto* was the start of another new chapter for Rush. While many fans appreciated Lifeson's return to the fore, Hine's production is still the subject of criticism from many.

The band themselves agree that while the material on *Presto* is worthy of appreciation, the final production was not as they had hoped. Geddy Lee explains:

> By the time we did *Presto*, I was getting sick of technology and wanted a return to a more basic approach. We were lucky that our producer, Rupert Hine, agreed, so that's why it's more about the vocals than anything else. However, I have to say that the album didn't turn out the way we hoped. If there's one album we'd love to do all over again, this is it. The songs are so much stronger than the way they came out.[1]

Despite its polarising effect on fans, the album sold well and provided Rush with another No. 1 single in 'Show Don't Tell'.

Songs

'Show Don't Tell'

Both a return to their roots and a progression towards a funk-metal-inspired contemporary sound, 'Show Don't Tell' is the album's confident opening statement. Featuring a complex heavy guitar riff as its central motif, it clearly marks Lifeson's return to the fore.

In his writing, Peart often employs a technique where he will use a phrase or saying and explore its multiple and sometimes unintended meanings. This phrase, 'Show Don't Tell', is often used by tutors of creative writing to encourage their students to do just that. Peart at the time was taking writing lessons, which would eventually lead to the publication of his first book, *The Masked Rider*. The song's lyric describes a court drama—a metaphor for the judgements we make upon others in our daily interactions. It is a warning to both the credulous and the charlatan: 'You can twist perceptions/Reality won't budge'.

Although the band had initially pledged to excise any synthetic elements from their new album, soft layers of keyboards make an appearance throughout the song. They are, however, relegated to a background supporting role and, in many cases, are not immediately obvious to the listener. While Lifeson's guitars dominate the track, Lee's lower register vocals shine through and an impressive funk bass solo towards the end of the track shows his continued influence on the modern Rush sound. Peart adapted to the band's new groove with apparently effortless ease and his typically thrilling drumming remains so on this album opener.

Only Rush's second No. 1 single in the USA, 'Show Don't Tell' was, appositely, the proof that many of Rush's original fans needed in order to return to the band they once loved.

'Chain Lightning'

Peart has previously described himself as a 'weather fanatic', and in this song, he has a chance to reference numerous weather phenomena to serve the song's lyric.[2] The premise of 'Chain Lightning' is that moments of wonder or beauty are amplified by the presence of another. While an individual may briefly respond to an event they have witnessed on their own, when someone else is there to share in it, 'The spark still flies/Reflected in another pair of eyes'.

Lifeson's guitar is still dominant here, and the unusual guitar solo is made more-so by the decision to completely reverse the part; perhaps one of the reasons this song has never been played live.

The interplay between the song's pop melodies and darker alternative-rock demonstrate the strength of Lee's and Lifeson's writing partnership. As Lifeson's pitch-shifted voice states at the song's close: 'That's nice'.

'The Pass'

Regarded by Lee as 'one of the best songs we've ever written', 'The Pass' is a slow and reflective song.[3] While it has little in common with most of Rush's most famous work, its tight focus on Lee's delivery of Peart's powerful lyric makes it a highlight of *Presto*, and—to the band at least—of their songwriting career.

The song, which deals with the subject of suicide, was particularly difficult for Peart to write. He compared the process to the writing of 'Manhattan Project', which involved an enormous amount of research. Peart himself has explained some of the process:

> I spent a lot of time on it, refining it, and, even more, doing research…. So I really worked hard to find true stores … what they felt, and why the people had taken this desperate step, and trying really hard fundamentally to understand something that to me is totally un-understandable. I wanted to de-mythologise it; take the nobility out of it. Let's not pretend it's a hero's end. It's not a triumph. It's a tragedy. It's a personal tragedy for them, but much more for the people left behind.[4]

While 'The Pass' is an unusually simple song for Rush, hints of their trademark sound are on offer to the listener with Peart's shuffling ride cymbal, Lee's use of punchy bass chords, and Lifeson's typically emotive guitar.

The lyric references Oscar Wilde's *Lady Windermere's Fan* with the line 'All of us get lost in the darkness/Dreamers learn to steer by the stars', but the most powerful literary allusion refers to the Bible. Lee's impassioned cry of Peart's perfectly chosen double meaning: 'Christ, what have you done?'

'War Paint'

In the opening crash of Lifeson's chords, the influence of Pete Townshend can once again be heard after many years of absence. 'War Paint' is another amalgamation of Rush's 1970s hard rock with the alternative-rock of the late 1980s. While there is little in the way of technicality, Lifeson does offer up some short musical surprises. Its driving beat and snappy melody make it an entertaining piece.

The lyric plays with the ideas of perception, particularly the gulf between how we are seen and how we would like to be seen—furthermore the steps we take to try to bridge that gap. Ultimately, the song is about integrity, and having the courage to accept ourselves as we are: 'Paint the mirror black/The mirror always lies'.

'Scars'

While initially the band intended to make *Presto* without the use of any electronic instruments, the temptation to do so proved too great. This is most noticeable on 'Scars'. While the intricate slapped bass groove may initially appear genuine, it is in fact a sequenced part. From the song's conception, the band intended it to have an unusual rhythmic feel. They even considered bringing in a session musician to enhance Peart's traditional drum parts with more exotic percussion. Eventually, by sampling the sounds required, Peart was able to perform the entire part without overdubbing a single drum. Much of the 'Scars' drum part has been adapted and incorporated into Peart's drum solos.

Peart's lyric is another that is a move towards more personally expressive writing. The 'scars' that the song refers to are a metaphor for hidden, and forgotten, memories. A place, a sound, or a smell can immediately return one to the moment the memory was formed: 'Scars of pleasure/Scars of Pain/Atmospheric changes make them sensitive again'.

In 'Scars', Peart makes mention, both in his drumming and lyrics, of his trip to West Africa, which he would later write about in his book *The Masked Rider*.

'Presto'

Showing once again that the band have not yet fully shaken off their electronic 1980s era, the clichéd whirl of a synthesizer can be heard opening 'Presto'. The song's simple chord progression fits with a lyric that at times does verge on silliness: 'If I could wave my magic wand/I'd make everything alright'. However, on closer inspection, the lyric contains numerous expressions of authentic wonder. The verses are a more mature approach to the magic of reality, 'I am made of the dust of the stars', while the pre-chorus returns to the childlike wish for super nature. The song explores the gap between wishes and reality and considers that while some of us do our best, most can do better. Confucius' saying 'It is better to radiate more light than heat' is referenced in the song, humbly revealing one of the author's own shortcomings.

While the album's title track begins with elements of soft folk-pop, the song provides plenty for the band's traditional rock fans as it develops into its blazing finale. A brilliantly succinct howling guitar solo from Lifeson precedes the song's final chorus.

While 'Presto' may initially seem platitudinous and in some ways pretentious, the band's history of artistic honesty, coupled with the lyric's detail makes it clear that care has been taken. 'Presto' rewards repeat listens and to many fans is a much more impressive track than is first apparent.

'Superconductor'

Nearly a decade after 'Spirit of Radio', 'Superconductor' is Peart's scathing attack on the banality and dishonesty of modern manufactured music. Peart's habit of redefining words is once again demonstrated here reimagining a 'Superconductor' as the invisible orchestrator of the performers under his control. The illusion of art is there, but the packaged popstars are nothing more than corporate puppets.

This up-beat, melodic rock song harks back to Rush's trademark use of covertly unusual time signatures. Like many of Rush's most commercial tracks, there is much more to the song than initially meets the eye. Thankfully, the underlying complexity did not deter DJs from playing the song that made the Top 40 in the US mainstream charts.

Rupert Hine's stamp is firmly placed on 'Superconductor' with a skilful amalgamation of technical heavy rock and lush synthesized pop. Hine also adds his name to the long list of Rush's musical collaborators with his layered backing vocals in the song's chorus.

'Anagram (for Mongo)'

Rush's sense of humour graduates from the liner notes to an actual song title here; the '(for Mongo)' suffix being a reference to the 'Candygram for Mongo' scene in *Blazing Saddles*. This playful reference is indicative of the song's content, which is effectively a word game turned into a lyric. The second half of each line is made up with letters from the first. The song, in an esoteric way, does make sense and some lines are quite effective regardless of their anagrammatic content: 'The night turns thin/The saint turns to sin'. However, limited by his wordplay, lines like 'Cosmic is largely comic' are somewhat jarring.

Musically, the song demonstrates Rush's continual determination to embrace the simpler side of writing, focusing less on technical prowess and much more on melody. This carefully arranged song is a brilliant example of Rush as pop-rock writers. Lee's decorative keyboards are extremely effective and a short piano solo is an unexpected treat.

When agreeing to produce Rush, Hine was keen to encourage Lee to adopt a lower, more traditional register for his vocals, arguing that this would make the performance of the lyric more believable. 'Anagram' is an excellent example of Hine's success in this regard.

'Red Tide'

In stark contrast to the preceding song, 'Red Tide' is an urgent and dramatic piece. Peart's piercing imagery is in perfect synergy with Lee and Lifeson's intense musical composition, which, layered with sharply synthesized horns and growling organ, is one of the most texturally interesting on the album.

While Peart had softly urged his listeners to consider ecological issues in 'Second Nature', 'Red Tide' is an unequivocal call to arms: 'THIS IS NOT A FALSE ALARM/THIS IS NOT A TEST'. With allusions to the AIDS virus, the depleted ozone layer, air pollution, and the song's eponymous natural phenomena, the song is full of the anger and frustration that have coloured much of Rush's most exciting work. Typically, the lyric finishes on a hopeful note: 'Now's the time to turn the tide/Now's the time to fight', before paraphrasing some of Dylan Thomas's most famous lines: 'Let us not go gently/To the endless winter night'.

Lifeson's guitar solos throughout *Presto* are short and highly punctuated pieces, but despite its brevity, his solo on 'Red Tide' is a deliberate attempt to capture the urgency and consequence of the song's lyrical content. It is this determination by the band to distil each theme to its fundamentals that makes 'Red Tide' a powerful and timelessly relevant song.

'Hand Over Fist'

Lifeson's sharp funk guitar provides some colour to this song's otherwise simple foundation. In a surprisingly effective turn, the song uses the imagery of rock-paper-scissors to make its universal point: a closed fist is defeated by an open hand. By opening up to the world and others in it, the world itself expands. Of course, things are never as simple as this, and the song is not shy about the anger and pride that make reconciliation so hard. The song's redemptive bridge section finds the narrator doing his best to put his insularity behind him: 'I feel my spirit resist/But I open up my fist'.

As well as his central rhythmic part, Lifeson's soaring guitar solo is another chance for him to shine on the album. Doubters would surely be persuaded by his stellar work on 'Hand Over Fist' that Rush—the guitar band—were back.

'Available Light'

A brooding slow-paced opening is coupled with the evocative imagery of urban canyons and howling winds that have 'seen' and 'heard all things'. Like many Rush songs, what at first appears to be a metaphor is in fact reality—as radio waves pass through us and the space around us all, carrying data. Despite this infinite information, it is not enough to bring the world to us in waves or digits—it has to be experienced for real, using the 'Available Light'.

The term 'Available Light' is used by photographers to describe shooting scenes without artificial lighting, and so it follows that Peart uses this analogy to explain his wish to experience things without filters or artificiality, but as they really are.

Lifeson adds to the song's slow groove and dark tonality with decorative bluesy licks, before suddenly breaking away into yet another brilliantly phrased emotive solo. With Peart loosening up and the band jamming on the song's motifs, the piece slowly fades away, ending the beginning of another new chapter in Rush history.

Interesting Liner Notes

Syme's monochrome art direction is, like the music, a move away from the overblown technicolour of the mid-80s, but ultimately leads the artwork to have a drab feel about it. The bizarre choice to feature a levitating rabbit on the front cover is still the subject of bewilderment from many fans.

The reduction in the use of synthesizers led necessarily to a diminished need for extra performers, but Hine—the sole additional musician—is credited for his background vocals and additional keyboards, as well as his production.

The magical theme is continued with 'A wave of the wand' and 'A tip of the magical hat' to the typically long list of helpers and encouragers.

The album is 'Brought to you by the letter D'.

14

Roll the Bones

Release date:	3 September 1991
Current edition:	Virgin/EMI CD
Additional keyboards and background vocals:	Rupert Hine

Recorded at Le Studio, Morin Heights, Quebec
Produced by Rupert Hine and Rush
Engineered by Stephen W. Tayler

Chart positions:	Canada: 11
	UK: 10
	US: 3

Consolidating the experimentation that had taken place on the transitional *Presto*, *Roll the Bones* is the band's second work to be produced by Rupert Hine. While the album continues the trend of keeping the arrangements guitar based, the vocals are undoubtedly the fundamental focus of all the songs. Recorded in 1991, contemporary pop music was saturated with a new wave of rap artists with honest lyrics quite different from the deliberately commercial work ordinarily peddled by record companies. Inspired by this, Peart incorporated some aspects of this style of beat-poetry into the lyrics throughout the album. Lee's vocal style, while retaining its melodic focus, does occasionally drift into an almost spoken-word delivery (not to mention the rap section in the album's title track).

After the anomaly of *Presto*, *Roll the Bones* restarts the trend of Rush producing albums with a single over-arching theme. Each song focuses on a different form of fortune, whether it is the literal luck of the dice, the luck one makes for themselves, or simply the chances that we all find by virtue of the place of our birth.

Of Rush's numerous stylistic eras, the two albums produced by Rupert Hine are almost an era within an era. While the band had deliberately moved towards their home-ground of hard rock, Hine's production had helped the band create a unique type of pop-rock, which is arguably the most commercially accessible of any Rush material.

Above left: The simple, yet highly effective cover for Rush's eponymous debut. (*Anthem Entertainment Group*)

Above right: John Rutsey, seen here in the centre, would appear solely on the band's 1974 debut LP before being replaced by Peart in the summer of that year. (*Anthem Entertainment Group*)

Below: The cover of *Fly by Night*, the first Rush album to feature the band's definitive line-up. (*Anthem Entertainment Group*).

Above: *Caress of Steel* was graphic designer Hugh Syme's first collaboration with the band. (*Anthem Entertainment Group*)

Below left: Syme's iconic cover for the band's 1976 album, *2112*. (*Anthem Entertainment Group*)

Below right: Keen to make a visual impact, though with little confidence in how to do so, the band, for a time, donned kimonos on stage. (*Anthem Entertainment Group*)

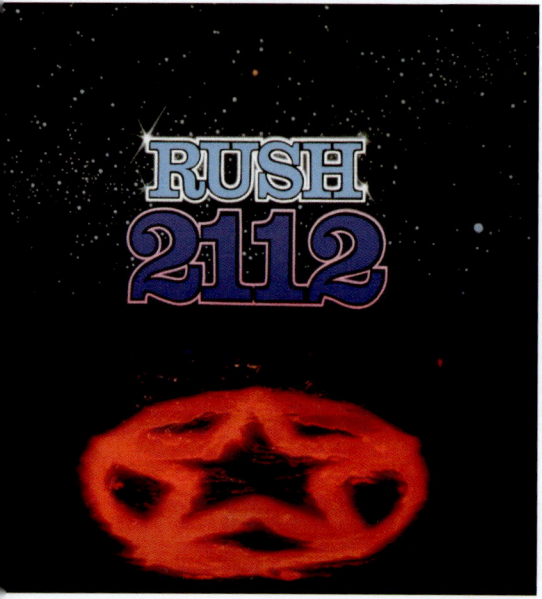

Above: Syme's fabulous *A Farewell to Kings* artwork foreshadows the visually complex style he would become famous for. (*Anthem Entertainment Group*)

Below left: The defiant 'star man' image became a motif for the band that would last throughout their career. Here it appears as part of the *A Farewell to Kings* artwork. (*Anthem Entertainment Group*)

Below right: An artistic representation of Apollo (left) and Dionysus (right) each keeping to their own hemisphere serves as the cover for 1978's *Hemispheres*. (*Anthem Entertainment Group*)

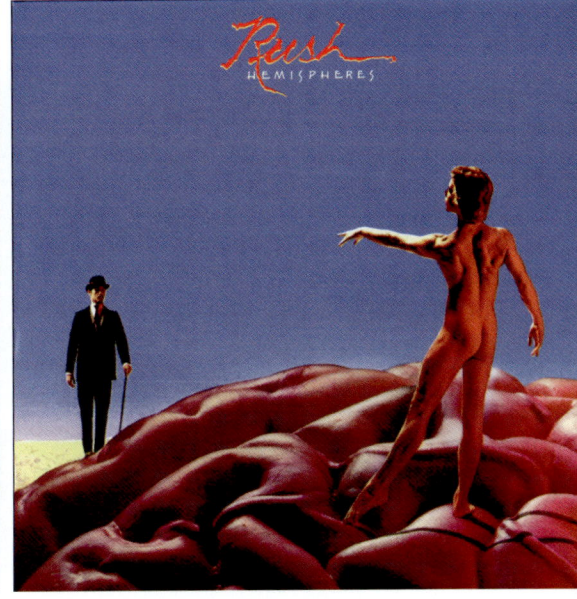

Above: The cover for *Permanent Waves* was subtly altered several times over various reissues. This is latest edition, with the newspaper headline and advertising boards altered. (*Anthem Entertainment Group*)

Below left: Rush's most commercially successful album and widely regarded as a high point in their career: 1981's *Moving Pictures*. (*Anthem Entertainment Group*)

Below right: Toronto's 'Department of Public Works' were thanked on the album inlay for providing the fire hydrant that appears here on the cover for *Signals*. (*Anthem Entertainment Group*)

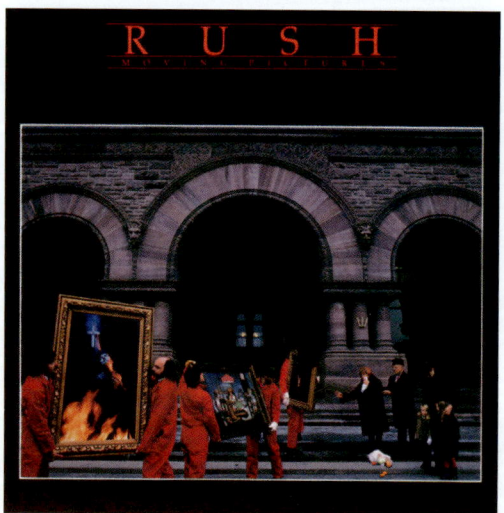

The double entendre on the album's front cover is given a third meaning on the rear of the inlay for *Moving Pictures*. (*Anthem Entertainment Group*)

This photograph, choreographed by Hugh Syme, was taken in front of the Ontario Legislative Building and was used to create one of Rush's most iconic album covers: *Moving Pictures*. (*Anthem Entertainment Group*)

Above: As a contrast to much of his recent work for the band, the cover for *Grace Under Pressure* features no photography and consists purely of a painting by Hugh Syme. (*Anthem Entertainment Group*)

Below left: Hugh Syme once again opts for a painting to depict several definitions of *Power Windows* for Rush's 1985 effort. (*Anthem Entertainment Group*)

Below right: Throughout his work with Rush, Hugh Syme had always created visually exciting and multi-layered artwork. 1987's *Hold Your Fire*, in stark contrast, features this subtle and minimalist cover. (*Anthem Entertainment Group*)

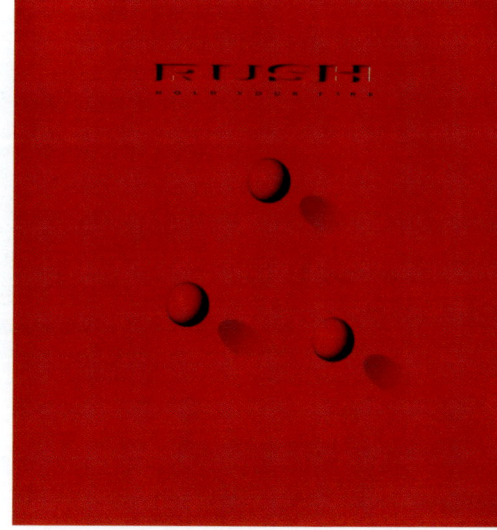

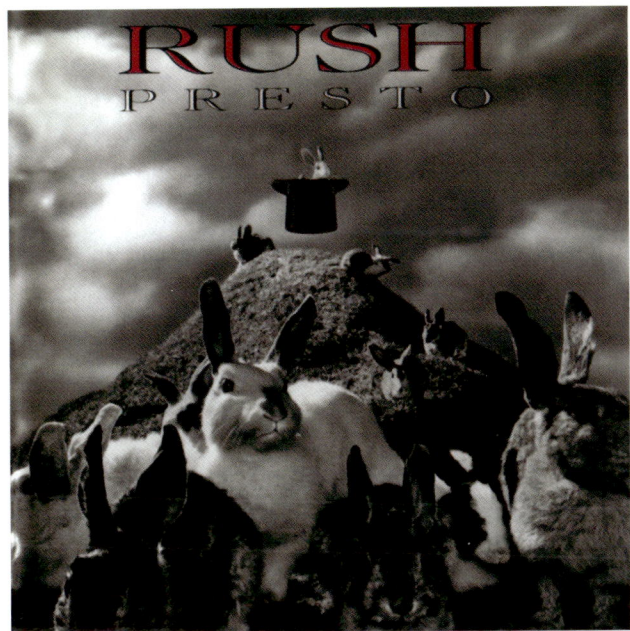

Above: The bizarre, monochrome, cunicular cover for 1989's *Presto*. (*Anthem Entertainment Group*)

Below left: Syme's cover for *Roll the Bones* won the 1992 Juno Award for best album cover design. It also prompted the following contact between a fan and Neil Peart via the Rush fan club: 'Q: Is the boy on the *Roll the Bones* cover Julian Lee?—Flavio de Assis, Brazil. A: Flavio, I'm only answering this because you're from Brazil. No'. (*Anthem Entertainment Group*)

Below right: 1993's *Counterparts* artwork was a simple but effective design. On the original CD release, the nut and bolt were printed on the plastic CD case itself with the artwork apparently disappearing when removing the inlay for closer inspection. (*Anthem Entertainment Group*)

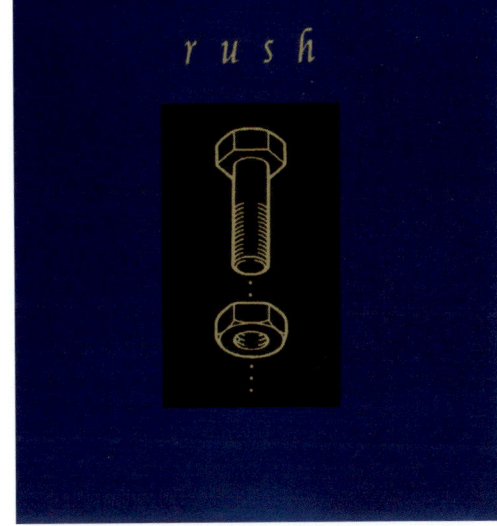

Above: Peart suggested using an Inukshuk, an Inuit sign-post structure that describes the shape of a human, as the cover for 1996's *Test for Echo*. Syme duly took note and created this formidable image. (*Anthem Entertainment Group*)

Below left: Septentrionalium Terrarum descriptio is a 1606 map of the North Pole: the first map of its kind ever made. Syme uses the subtly edited map here as inlay art for the *Test for Echo* album. (*Anthem Entertainment Group*)

Below right: Syme's painting for the cover of 2002's comeback album *Vapor Trails* captures the furious energy and intensity of the album's music. (*Anthem Entertainment Group*)

Above: The cover for 2007's *Snakes and Arrows* depicts Leela—the two millennia-old Buddhist game of self-knowledge and precursor to the board game *Snakes and Ladders*. (*Anthem Entertainment Group*)

Below left: 2012's *Clockwork Angels* depicts a clock face whose numbers have been replaced by alchemic symbols. The hands on the clock show the time as 9.12, which—in the evening—is, of course, 2112. (*Anthem Entertainment Group*)

Below right: The story of *Clockwork Angels* takes place in a 'steampunk' universe—an alternate reality where steam is the predominant power of all machines. Here a steam liner travels above a rough sea. (*Anthem Entertainment Group*)

Above: 'The Body Electric' was released as a single in 1984. A limited run were printed on translucent red vinyl. (*Mitch Simpson*)

Below: A limited edition picture disc of 1978's *Hemispheres*. (*Mitch Simpson*)

A ticket for 1978's *A Farewell to Kings* tour. *Hemispheres* would be released less than half a year later. (*Tim Starace*)

Above: A ticket for 1980's *Moving Pictures* mini warm-up tour. (*Tim Starace*)

Below: A ticket for the band's *Exit...Stage Left* tour of 1981. This particular concert was infamous for a riot that occurred outside the venue beforehand. Supposedly, Peart was late arriving to the venue, which delayed the doors opening. Subsequently, rioting fans were tear-gassed by police. (*Tim Starace*)

The dedication and enthusiasm of Rush fans is well known and proven here by this impressive tattoo. (*Mitch Simpson*)

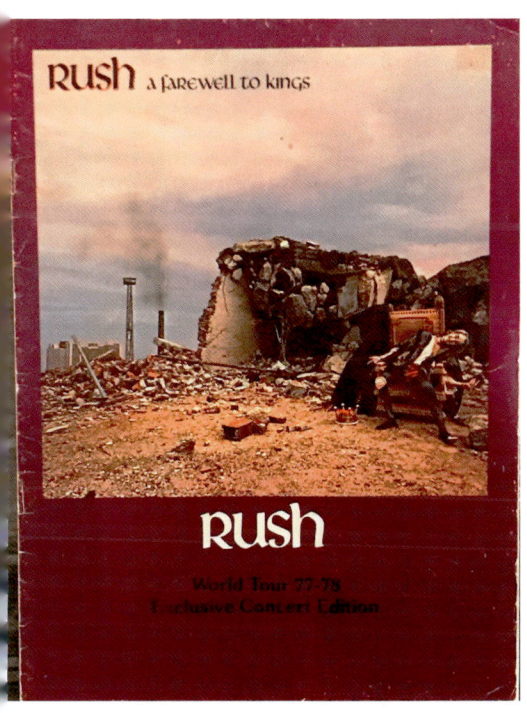 

Above left: A souvenir tour book from Rush's 1977–78 *A Farewell to Kings* tour. (*Tim Starace*)

Above right: A full-page advert was taken out in *Sounds* magazine in June 1980 to advertise Rush's back catalogue. (*Author*)

Right: A souvenir tour book from Rush's *Hemispheres* tour of 1978–79. (*Tim Starace*)

Above: A souvenir tour book from Rush's *Snakes and Arrows Live* tour of 2007–08. (*Alex Dunbar*)

Below: Rush's tour books were of a good standard throughout their career, featuring humorous and interesting pieces written by the band, as well as high-quality photography such as this. (*Alex Dunbar*)

Rush performing live at the Ziggo Dome, Amsterdam, Netherlands 2 June 2013 as part of their *Clockwork Angels Live* Tour. (*Sebastiaan van Stijn*)

The *Clockwork Angels Live* tour would prove to be the final Rush tour to come to Europe. Here, the band perform at the Ziggo Dome, Amsterdam. (*Sebastiaan van Stijn*)

Howard Ungerleider's spectacular light shows would continue to impress fans throughout the band's career. Here, the stage of the O2 Arena in London is flooded with colour on 24 May 2013. (*Sebastiaan van Stijn*)

Live at the O2 Arena, Greenwich, London, on 24 May 2013 for the *Clockwork Angels Live* tour. (*Sebastiaan van Stijn*)

Roll the Bones would be the last time the band would work with Hine, but with its intelligent lyrics and carefully crafted songs, it is an album whose songs would remain popular with fans and remain in the band's live performances for years to come.

Songs

'Dreamline'

This confident opener was the album's lead single and peaked at No. 1 in the US mainstream rock charts. Lee's lower vocal register is brought to the fore while performing a lyric that drifts between the terrestrial imagery of day-to-day life and the awesome abstractions of dreams. Whether these dreams become reality is—in concert with the album's theme—a matter of luck and indeed whether chances that present themselves are taken. Deep into their career with thirteen albums behind them, the line 'We're only immortal for a limited time' is apt, though certainly premature with regard to the band's career.

Peart's drumming brings an urgency and energy into a song that is otherwise carried largely by Lee's vocals. The arrangement, which features a minimum of musical extravagance, is a case of distilled and efficient songwriting. The piece is a simple and powerful opener with a satisfying lyric.

'Bravado'

From the urgent hope of 'Dreamline', the listener is taken immediately to the mournful 'Bravado'. This requiem for broken dreams and lost battles remains, despite its sorrowful tone, hopeful. We can lick our wounds, dust ourselves off, and persist: 'We will pay the price/But we will not count the cost'. This line, taken with permission from John Barth's *Tidewater Tales*, is the song's second literary allusion after the song's first line, which references the mythical Icarus and his fatal hubris.

The band themselves regard the song as one of their best marriages of lyric and music and have each separately referred to it as one of their favourites on the album. Peart later took inspiration from his own lyric after a disappointing experience taking part in a Buddy Rich tribute concert. Technical failures and a lack of rehearsal tempted Peart to cut ties with any such project again, but, remembering 'Bravado', he decided to organise the Buddy Rich tribute album *Burning for Buddy*. He refers to this as 'the first time I had ever been inspired by my own words!'[1]

Lifeson's guitar work is also notable in that much of it was taken from the relatively low-quality demo tapes. Lifeson also ended up keeping the guitar solo despite its initial function as a simple placeholder:

When we're developing the arrangement in the writing stages, I toss a solo on tape so we have something to listen to. Its late at night, the lights are down low, and I'm by myself. These were supposed to be throwaway solos, but when it was time to do the 'real' solos, Neil had already adjusted his parts to fit what I'd played. So it came down to me trying to recreate everything—which doesn't work. You might improve the sound, but even if you play exactly the same notes you'll never capture that magic feel. The solos in 'Ghost of a Chance' and 'Bravado' are certainly my favourites on the record, if not among my favourite solos ever. When I listen to them, I hear the way I felt at that time. That's really the key.[2]

'Roll the Bones'

One of the band's most successful experiments in genre fusion features moments of rock, funk, folk, and, famously, rap. The lyric is one that accepts the existence of free will but also that no one's destiny is ever entirely their own decision. There are always unexpected events that can help or hinder us and while we like to take credit for our own success, we tend to blame our failures on external influence: 'Winners take that praise/Losers seldom take that blame'.

While there are some unanswerable questions, 'Why are we here?/Because we're here', and we certainly cannot predict our future, the song is a battle cry of encouragement to the hesitant or fearful: we do not know what will happen, but give it a try, take a chance: 'Roll the bones'.

While the band were not necessarily fans of the musicality of the genre, Peart had taken influence from the writing of rap acts such as LL Cool J and Public Enemy. Peart was surprised when Lee and Lifeson agreed to try and incorporate one of his rap-influenced lyrics into the song. The band took a great deal of time to decide who would perform the part and considered hiring a professional rapper, a female vocalist, the Canadian musician Robby Robertson and even Monty Python's John Cleese. Although most of the potential performers were interested in recording the part, the band ultimately opted for the pitch-shifted voice of Geddy Lee, which the band agrees has a longevity that many of the other options would have lacked.

'Face Up'

Exchanging metaphors from dice to cards, 'Face Up' continues the album's theme of luck and the way we react to the chances that we find.

With hints of funk, pop, and, unexpectedly, country making their way into the song, it is one that the band ultimately felt was less than the sum of its parts. Peart's furiously upbeat drumming blasts are ahead of the rest of the band, who sound somewhat pedestrian behind his impressive performance.

'Where's My Thing?'

Their first standalone instrumental to be recorded in over a decade, 'Where's My Thing?' retains the intense complexity, unusual time signatures, and sudden changes of timbre that characterise all of Rush's instrumentals. However, the piece is unique in its exposition of Peart's passion for jazz drumming: backed by synthesized horns, Peart suddenly adopts a fast swing-groove and puts his jazz influences to good use. While the piece is characterised by its early '90s production and the significant use of decorative keyboards, it is nevertheless a worthy addition to Rush's instrumental canon.

In 1992, 'Where's My Thing?' was the second of Rush's works to fail to win the Grammy for Best Instrumental Rock Performance. The band were glad to lose to their friend and opening act for part of the *Roll the Bones* tour, Eric Johnson with his piece 'Cliffs of Dover'.

The subtitle 'Part IV, "Gangster of Boats" Trilogy' is, in fact, as nonsensical as it initially appears.

'The Big Wheel'

The subtle country influence that was hinted at on 'Face Up' is fully realised in this song. Lee somehow succeeds in his vocal delivery, performing the verses like a weathered troubadour—another of the band's experiments with a more conversational approach to vocal performance.

Tackling the enormous subjects of work, faith, failure, and love, framed once again within the theme of fortune, this song is an example of Peart's newly favoured technique of writing what are apparently more personal lyrics in order to cover the grander subjects of humanity. Despite the sense of revelation, Peart has explained that while many of his lyrics appear to be autobiographical, they are almost all written from the point of view of a fictional character.

Although the song is one of the simplest in Rush's entire catalogue, teetering on the brink of being a run of the mill pop song, the lyric holds numerous treats for the curious listener. The final bridge section of the song subtly switches the words in two common phrases to create the brilliantly multi-dimensional 'twist of faith' and 'leap of fate'.

'Heresy'

Written in response to the dismantling of the Berlin Wall and the subsequent failure of the Soviet Union and Warsaw Pact, 'Heresy' is perhaps the angriest lyric Peart has ever put to paper. 'Heresy' is powerful in its frustrated surrender: there is nothing to do except move on. Years of Cold War fear, suffering, and poverty have ruined the lives of millions and wasted untold fortune on military build-up—all for ideology's sake, and now it is over, 'who will pay?'

While the first two verses deal with the very real suffering that those behind the Iron Curtain had to endure, the final verse refers to Peart's own experience as a child being told about Canada's potential involvement in a nuclear war: 'All the crap we had to take/Bombs and basement fallout shelters/All our lives at stake'. The final sentence subtly referencing the song's relevance to the album's overall theme of chance.

Countering the furious lyric is a relatively laid-back, somewhat sombre piece of music with Lifeson's singing guitar providing the solace to an otherwise dark piece. The drums are inspired by a particular beat that Peart heard on his travels in West Africa. This pattern was later incorporated into one of Peart's solo pieces: 'Momo's Dance Party'.

'Ghost of a Chance'

While Rush have generally avoided the cliché of the traditional love song, 'Ghost of a Chance' approaches the subject of love from a logical perspective—considering the almost infinite number of different paths that two people may take away from each other—and yet, that couples still find each other, love each other, and stay together.

Switching between an upbeat blues groove in the verse through to a laid-back and string-laden chorus, the song is a fine example of Rush's use of light and shade in their songs. A brilliantly expressive solo from Lifeson is the only break from the standard verse–chorus structure of this extremely simple but well-crafted song, which Peart regards as 'one of our all time good ones'.

This was another rare hit single for Rush, hitting the No. 1 spot in the US rock radio charts.

'Neurotica'

Showing once again that they have still not quite shed their passion for electronic music, 'Neurotica' features a repeating sequenced bass-synth as well as numerous additional layers of keyboards. The crisp-hard rock that colours the rest of the album soon reappears however in the fast-paced chorus section.

The lyric is a frustrated look at the neuroses that so often spoil the day-to-day life of so many people. The lyric suggests that many are so crippled by insecurity and fear that they find themselves unable to do anything about it. Peart, however, makes clear the gravity of the situation: 'Life is a diamond you turn into dust' and firmly urges these people to get on with life and make it work.

The casual phrasing of the lyric is an oddity in Peart's canon ('Baby, don't you ask yourself why?'), and is almost jarring in some places. While 'Neurotica', save for a blistering solo from Lifeson, is a relatively bland piece, it is nevertheless another of the band's worthy experiments.

'You Bet Your Life'

Taking its title from the Groucho Marx game-show, this fast-paced rocker exposes the sometimes uncomfortable truth that in every single decision we make we are betting a little portion of our life on it: betting that it will be the best chance we can take, the best decision we can make.

The multi-layered vocal in the chorus made the track one of the most difficult to arrange and mix in the studio, but ultimately this spoken-word backing vocal adds a brilliant harmonic foundation to the chorus and, with its compelling imagery, is perhaps a more successful use of the rap influence by the band.

The rapid guitar-led groove that drives the track coupled with Peart's busier drum parts make this return to unadulterated rock a thrilling finale to the album. 'You Bet Your Life' virtually abandons electronic decoration in favour of the band's traditional staples of bass, drums, and guitar. An exciting and powerful end to the album and an intriguing hint of what is to come.

Interesting Liner Notes

After the monochromatic art on *Presto*, the brilliant imagery within the album booklet and the iconic album cover make *Roll the Bones* another of Hugh Syme's great successes.

Additional keyboards and background vocals are credited to Rupert Hine, though no other additional musicians play on the album. Lifeson, however, provides backing vocals for the first time since the band's début.

Special thanks are extended to 'those who keep us "rolling"', including 'the psychedelic shack', 'the sugar shack', Mr. Big (band and crew) and 'to our families who are always there to catch us when we stop rolling'.

The album is 'Brought to you by the letter "B"'.

The notes are concluded by a short and cryptic phrase 'Now it's dark'—a reference to the David Lynch film *Blue Velvet*.

15

Counterparts

Released: 19 October 1993
Current edition: Virgin/EMI CD
Additional keyboards: John Webster
Recorded at Le Studio, Morin Heights, Quebec
Produced by Peter Collins and Rush
Recorded by Kevin (Caveman) Shirley
Mixed by Michael Letho assisted by Simon Pressey and Brett Zilahi
Chart positions: Canada: 6
UK: 14
US: 2

While the two preceding albums had succeeded in removing the layers of synthesizers that had come to dominate Rush's sound in the '80s, they had been replaced with an unusual pop production that Rupert Hine had encouraged the band to explore. While Hine's work as a producer moved the band towards the avant-garde sound he had himself developed as a performer previously, Rush were perhaps in need of support in their organic development rather than a sudden and arguably contrived shift led by a producer. Consequently, the band, keen to fully realise their desire to work as a traditional rock band again, persuaded Peter Collins to return as their producer.

During the *Roll the Bones* tour, the band became aware that their recent albums had not captured much of the power or energy of their impressive live sound and were committed to rectifying this on the next album. Consequently, they hired Kevin Shirley as studio engineer. His apposite nickname 'Caveman' was attributed to his simple approach to using high-quality microphones to record as much music 'as live' as possible, thus creating an organic sound with a genuine live feel.

Counterparts succeeds in this regard being one of the most sonically satisfying Rush albums ever produced while still retaining the dynamic range and audio fidelity that would begin to lack in future work by the band. The songs themselves are a stylistic response to the grunge and alternative-rock that had begun to dominate the rock scene of the early 1990s. The pop and hip-hop influences had run their course: *Counterparts* was Rush's development into their purest and most powerful distillation—back again as a genuine power-trio.

Counterparts is regarded by many fans as a return to form by Rush. While the band intended to return to their power-trio roots with *Presto* four years earlier, it is, arguably, with *Counterparts* that they belatedly achieved their aim. Collins' influence as producer cannot be overstated and the album's enormous rock sound is a huge part of its success.

The excision of synthesizers and a more organic production have helped the album remain fresh in later years and it has, arguably, dated considerably better than many of its recent predecessors. One of the band's most successful albums, *Counterparts* peaked at No. 2 in the USA.

Counterparts would be the last Rush album to be recorded at the now derelict 'Le Studio' in Morin Heights.

Songs

'Animate'

As if to ensure to the listeners that Hine's crystalline and arguably sterile productions had been consigned to history, 'Animate' opens with an audible count-in from Peart before the raw power of his Ludwig kit dominates the soundscape. Lee shortly joins in with one of the first expositions of the technique that would dominate his playing from *Counterparts* onwards: the fast and percussive flamenco finger-style that allows him to lay down the bass part with an enormous amount of rhythmic expression.

The song explores the psychological ideas of Karl Jung who posited that each of us has a masculine and feminine subconscious: the Animus and Anima respectively. While 'Animate' appears initially to be about two people, or indeed one person's reaction to another, it is in fact about the way men respond to their own feminine subconscious—a tempering influence which must be gently dominated in order that it serves its function, but also that it does not overwhelm one's personality entirely.

While the song's main rhythmic theme has its roots in British R&B, the ethereal mid-section was heavily influenced by some of the tribal drumming that Peart had heard on his travels in Africa.

'Stick It Out'

With its lyric—a simple exploration of the title's double meaning—the song that the band claim 'verges on parody' is one of the heaviest the band would record.

With guitars tuned down to Drop D, Lee and Lifeson provide the key motif of the song in its uncomplicated, heavy riff. While the riff is itself straightforward, its ambiguous rhythmic placement is the first hint that this song is significantly more complex than it initially seems. With its jazzy interlude and complex percussive turnarounds, 'Stick it Out' is considerably more interesting than its simple hard-rock tropes may initially suggest. While the band have spoken somewhat unkindly about the song, they did go on to perform it live during their retrospective *Time Machine* tour, suggesting that some fondness does remain for this swaggeringly heavy track.

'Stick it Out' has the dubious honour of being the only Rush song to have been critiqued by MTV's *Beavis and Butthead*, who were unimpressed with the song's promo-video and its star, 'a dude with dreadlocks and tattoos strapped to a chair'.

'Cut to the Chase'
Counterparts continues to bare its teeth with this straight ahead groove-rocker. In this song, Rush, continuously taking influence from their contemporaries, channel the alternative-rock that was so popular in the early 1990s.

Lyrically, the song is another of Peart's self-assured rages against the norm—an expression of his irrepressible drive to chase after dreams and desires: 'You may be right/It's all a waste of time/I guess that's just a chance I'm prepared to take'.

Lifeson's lively guitar solo takes its influence from Eric Johnson, fluidly gliding from note to note at an impressive pace, once again proving to any doubters that Lifeson's technical ability equals his impressive creativity.

'Nobody's Hero'
While this song's overall sound is considerably lighter than the rest of *Counterparts*, its theme is extremely dark. Each of the song's two verses relays a story of the tragic death of an ordinary, unremarkable person. The song suggests that perhaps the value we put on human life is unreasonably skewed to those who are idolised for banal achievements. The song insists the listener evaluates his own heroes: while 'the champion player/who plays the perfect game' may well be worshipped by his fans, perhaps true heroism is in 'the pride of purpose/in the unrewarding job'. Peart's cynical, yet ultimately hopeful lyric is critical of the monetisation and glorification of celebrity culture, but also considers the other side: the numerous unrecognised heroes in our daily midst.

Lifeson performs the verses of this song on an acoustic guitar in the highly strung 'Nashville tuning', giving the song its light and folky feel.

'Between the Sun and Moon'
Alex Lifeson describes this song as 'a tribute to the '60s' and with its muted fingered guitar, bluesy groove, and flailing drum part, it is plain to hear. The unusual lyric, with its psychedelic, pseudo-religious overtones, helps continue

this theme. Another collaboration with the often inscrutable Pye Dubois, his bizarre imagery adds an air of authenticity to this fiery homage.

The song is something of a showcase for Lifeson's guitar playing, through which he channels many influential guitar players including Keith Richards and Pete Townshend. The song's bridge is a clear attempt to capture the energy and excitement of The Who at their heavy best, something that, owing to their exuberant enthusiasm, Rush succeed in.

'Alien Shore'

One of Lee's most adventurous basslines on the album—a dark and rapidly shifting spectre beneath its counterpart: Lifeson's glittering arpeggiating guitar. Switching between steady hard rock chord progressions and alt-rock funk grooves, 'Alien Shore' is a musical feast that perfectly reflects the lyric's theme of the 'other' and how we respond to it.

It is another of Peart's lyrics that could so easily have slipped into platitude but does not. With its realistic view of the world, and acceptance that there is a gulf to cross before mutual respect and understanding can be attained, the song acts as a map and not a guidebook.

This song's title may have been influenced by the album *Alien Shores* by the Canadian band Platinum Blonde. Lifeson had collaborated with this band on numerous occasions, and was influenced at the time to incorporate some of their new-wave style into Rush's sound during the mid-1980s.

For reasons that are unapparent, 'Alien Shore' begins with the sound of Lifeson squeezing his nostrils shut and half-singing the words: 'Out of my nose'.

'The Speed of Love'

This mid-tempo song is Peart's attempt to de-mythologise romantic love and is an attempt to shed some light on how fleeting and complex love really is—as opposed to the fictional world of love that exists only in books, film, and pop music.

Peart's drums occupy the background throughout the piece, but feature an impressive amount of detail when listened to carefully, providing decoration to areas of the song that would otherwise remain empty. Lee and Lifeson now take a step back and allow the vocal to shine through, notwithstanding the addition a very simple textural guitar solo.

'Double Agent'

While Rush had, by this time, largely left their 'progressive' label behind them, 'Double Agent' harks back to their early work and its fusion between complex rhythmic work and powerful hard rock. Described by Lee as 'a complete exercise in self-indulgence', the song has an intensity and joyful exuberance that the band had not captured in the studio for many years. Written towards the end of the *Counterparts*' sessions, the piece was designed as a vehicle for the band to let themselves go and escape from some of the more constraining arrangements on the rest of the album.

The lyric is an expression of exhausted dilemma and uses the imagery of espionage and spy novels to describe two sides battling for dominance of an unsure mind. The final verse describes the clarity of mind that so often appears after a good night's sleep. Perhaps not a very rock 'n' roll moral to the fable, but this is Rush after all.

'Double Agent' is another of Rush's songs to feature a spoken part by Geddy Lee—another quirky addition to this spirited song.

'Leave That Thing Alone'
This instrumental continues where 'Where's My Thing?' left off with its funky bass and drum interplay, though the synthesizers and big-band influence have been largely excised in favour of a more avant-garde jazz influence. Peart also incorporates his take on Nigerian-style drumming in this constantly changing piece. Lifeson's singing guitar provides respite from the intense rhythm section and soars over the instrumental's melodic refrain.

While this piece has little in common with the band's older material, the smack of wood blocks that gave even more character to 'YYZ' can also be heard on this track.

'Cold Fire'
While this song was eventually regarded by the band of one of their favourites on the album, it did not come together easily. The lyric—which presents a conversation between a potential romantic couple—is unusual territory for the band and it was extremely difficult for them to find the right sort of feel for the piece. Lee explains: 'You want to make sure it doesn't sound trite or hackneyed or you're not just doing yet another song about relationships'. The band credit Collins' excellent production for helping to craft the song into its final form and giving it the space and atmosphere needed for Lee's raconteur-ish delivery.

'Cold Fire', following on from 'The Speed of Love', is a song that Peart uses to further debunk the lore of love songs. The female character in the song (who is the more astute of the two characters) at one point states: 'This is not a love song/ This isn't fantasy land'.

Lifeson is once again at the fore of the piece with his explosive main riff and disputatious guitar solo. Lee's performance of this complex lyric succeeds in portraying its story in a genuine way while maintaining the melodic centre of the song.

'Everyday Glory'
While Peart's political and philosophical views had developed enormously since his pro-objectivist work in the 1970s, this uplifting and hopeful song contains the distilled and refined remnants of these earlier views. In 'Everyday Glory', Peart encourages each of us to be our own hero and take responsibility for our own lives, but also to be the light in the dark—to be the good we wish to see in the world.

The heart-breaking image of a disintegrating family in the first verse is emotive imagery that whether taken at face value or as a metaphor has a clear message, we all make mistakes and we all experience suffering, but we must all, like the mythical phoenix, rise from the ashes and carry on.

The lyric to the second verse is reminiscent of 'Subdivisions' with its imagery of boredom and uniformity. Here, Peart gives credit to those silent and largely invisible positive motivators that helped him and others like him escape his confines and achieve his dreams: 'Just one spark of decency/Against a starless night/One glow of hope and dignity/A child can follow the light'.

'Everyday Glory' is a song that presents a difficult truth in a motivating and encouraging way: it may be that we really are on our own and that nobody is coming to our aid, it may be that the world really does owe us nothing, but it is for these reasons that we have to be even more determined in our resolve: 'If the future's looking dark/We're the ones who have to shine/If there's no one in control/We're the ones who draw the line/Though we live in trying times/We're the ones who have to try/Though we know that time has wings/We're the ones who have to fly'.

While the music edges close to the realms of cliché, the integrity that Rush have so obviously maintained in their previous work makes this song convincing in its honesty; thus, what could have fallen flat as a trite motivational piece comes across to most listeners as a brilliantly uplifting song.

Peart's inspiration for 'Everyday Glory' came, like many of his lyrics, from his travels. While many cynics disagree, this song stems from his belief that 'in all neighbourhoods of the world ... the heroes still outnumber the villains'.[1]

Interesting Liner Notes

Syme's impressive work for the band continues with an almost impossibly large number of literal counterparts displayed throughout the album booklet; some are more carefully hidden than others. One of the early CD releases had the nut and bolt from the front cover printed on the plastic case itself so that on removing the album's booklet, the album art seemed to disappear.

The album features a small number of additional musicians: John Webster is credited for playing additional keyboards while the notable composer Michael Kamen arranged and conducted the orchestration on 'Nobody's Hero'.

The 'primate' who is featured in the album's booklet is not credited, while his keepers, 'Monkey Business', are.

'Assistance, inspiration comic relief and/or just plain friendly service' was provided by (among others) 'Mr. Big, Eric Johnson, Gamera (is turtle meat), *The Larry Sanders Show*, 417 TAC Squadron, *midi Scoozeball*', and 'our counterweights and counterparts: our families'.

The album is 'brought to you by the letter "œ"'.

The album is in memory of Pat Lynes and Lee Tenner.

Test for Echo

Release date: 10 September 1996
Current edition: Virgin/EMI CD
Recorded at Bearsville Studios, Bearsville, New York
Produced by Peter Collins and Rush
Recorded by Cliff Norrell
Mixed by Andy Wallace
Chart positions: Canada: 3
UK: 25
US: 5

Released nearly three years after *Counterparts*, *Test for Echo* marked the end of the longest break the band had given themselves since Rush's formation. While Lee spent the time with his young family and pursuing his personal interests, Lifeson let loose with his solo project. Peart, relentlessly determined to improve himself, entirely altered his drumming style after intense instruction from legendary jazz drumming tutor Freddy Gruber. Peart, who had always drummed using matched grip, began to play using traditional grip and deliberately drummed with a looser feel.

Peter Collins once again returned to produce the album, bringing with him the heavy alternative-rock sound that was so effective on *Counterparts*; however, *Test for Echo* is often criticised for lacking the excitement and cohesiveness that the band's previous albums had been lauded for.

With its powerful Peter Collins production, *Test for Echo* may initially sound like the sequel to its predecessor, *Counterparts*. Closer inspection reveals, however, that while *Counterparts* drew on the Rush's love of the so-called British Invasion bands of the 1960s, *Test for Echo* is an album that reflects the contemporary alternative-rock bands of the 1990s. Consequently, *Test for Echo* sounds more dated than its predecessor, whose timeless influences are still in vogue to this day.

Despite its occasionally thrilling riffs, *Test for Echo* sees Lifeson returning to the role of soundscape architect—applying his sonic textures as a backdrop to

Lee's prominent vocal melodies. Peart, despite his new drumming technique, is arguably more laid-back than ever, while Lee's work on the album is as a singer and songwriter first and bassist second. Consequently, the album, while mature, features little of the youthful exuberance that excited many Rush fans at the beginning of their career.

Test for Echo would be the final Rush studio album before the great hiatus during which many, including the band themselves, believed that Rush would never play again. It is, even more so than any other Rush album, the end of an era.

Songs

'Test for Echo'

A wild and contrasting mixture of styles are carefully stitched together to construct the album's title track. The manic time-changing riffs and loose, melodic verses provide a thrilling opener that incorporates much of the band's earlier stylistic influence, as well as the heavy alternative-rock style of the mid-'90s.

The song's lyric was yet another collaboration between Peart and Pye Dubois. Dubois's lyrics are often impenetrable to understanding but are, this time, quite clear. The song is a harsh commentary on the real-time media world of 'infotainment' news, the modern-day freak shows of early 'reality TV', and the commercialisation of absolutely everything.

Despite the fact the lyric has a clarity that much of Dubois' other work lacks, this does not hinder the song's unusual and beautiful imagery: 'Camera curves over caved-in cop cars'.

The song's title, 'Test for Echo', is a request for feedback. An attempt to ask if anyone else's feelings reflect our own—or as Peart himself put it: '"Excuse me, does anybody else think this is weird? Am I weird?" While the answer to those questions might be "Yes!" it's good to know that you're not the only one, that you're not alone'.[1]

'Driven'

This riff-based alt-rock piece once again connects the heavier and darker sound of Rush with Lee's melodic vocals. Despite the changes of time signature and gradual textural development, the song's constant repetition of its short riff does, arguably, make the song overlong and perhaps under-edited.

Lee originally demoed the song with three bass tracks—the additional two to stand in for Lifeson's rhythm guitar. Lifeson, pleased with the arrangement, suggested that Lee keep all three basses in the final version in addition to Lifeson's guitar. This idea met with Lee's enthusiastic approval and so 'Driven' remains one of Rush's most heavily textured guitar-based pieces.

The simple, but pleasing lyric uses driving as a metaphor for life: the balance between taking control of our own lives and allowing others to take the strain. The multiple meanings and contexts of the word 'driven' make the relatively simple lyric more effective. Ultimately, and unsurprisingly, Peart suggests that it is a far better thing to be in control of oneself and indeed to take responsibility for one's own life: 'It's my turn to drive'.

'Half the World'

The shortest song on the album and a minor hit for the band, 'Half the World' peaked at No. 6 on the US *Billboard* Mainstream Rock Chart.

Primarily a vehicle for Peart's lyric, the song is a simple, melody driven folk-rock work. On the track, Lifeson can be heard performing acoustic guitar and mandola as well as electric guitar.

While Peart had travelled throughout the world as a musician, perhaps his international state of mind really began to take hold after his bicycle travels—many of which were quite literally off the beaten track. His travels through China and Africa brought him into contact with ways of life that were unfathomably modest in comparison to those which are commonplace elsewhere. It is unsurprising then that Peart chose to write a song about 'how the other half live'. Pleasingly, the song's lyric does not split the world neatly in two. Depending on the qualities mentioned, an entirely different part of the world springs to mind. Although there may have been a temptation to split the world into the wealthy West and the suffering East, the song brings to mind the rich, the poor, the proud, the modest, the waxing, and the waning, and all in the form of different places and peoples. Thus, it is in this mishmash of characteristics that the song gradually patches together the entire world and shows—without too much cliché—that we are all one people.

'The Color of Right'

This mid-tempo piece has little of the frenetic energy or complex musical ideas that Rush fans had come to expect. While the layered guitars provide a loud wall of sound, the light-hearted melodies and pulled back drums make this another of the band's forays into pop-rock.

'The Color of Right' is often used as a legal term in the UK and Commonwealth countries (including Canada) and is a defence used when somebody breaks a law without any intention to do so, or without knowledge that what they were doing was wrong; this song speaks of that in a general moral way, criticising the legalistic and bureaucratic: 'I'm so full of what is right/I can't see what is good'.

Peart's interest in science is also put to good use in the lyric with a particularly effective double meaning: 'Gravity and distance change the passage of light/ Gravity and distance change the color of right'.

'Time and Motion'

With its aggressive guitars and brooding melody, 'Time and Motion' is another track that clearly takes its influence from the modern alt-rock scene. With numerous time signatures and floods of heavy guitar, the track brings to mind emerging bands of the time such as Tool and Primus.

While the song quickly changes from part to part, the tonal quality of the song remains fairly constant throughout. The song features little melodic movement, and at over five minutes, it is arguably another example of an overlong and under-edited track. Despite these potential flaws, Lifeson's guitar solo is powerful and aggressive as it brings to mind the cosmic chaos to which the song refers.

From 'gravity and distance' in the preceding song to 'Time and Motion', the lyric refers to the effect that these physical ideas have on our experiences and emotions. Whether metaphorically or in reality, we are all constantly in motion and everything we experience affects us differently depending on who and where we are at the time. Great, yet distant bodies interact in profound ways. 'The mighty ocean/Dances with the moon', they affect each other instantaneously.

'Totem'

This playful folky track is a considerably lighter reflection on religion than the scathing attacks that Peart would deliver on *Snakes and Arrows* a decade later. Nevertheless, it is an indicator of his deeply sceptical attitude towards it. After listing aspects of multitudinous ancient faiths, Peart goes on to compare the role of modern media to that of organised religion. His deep cynicism regarding both is plain to see.

Lifeson's subtle textural work on the song is one of its most interesting aspects. Soft Celtic melodies and swirling harmonics add something of a transcendent layer to this proudly terrestrial song.

'Dog Years'

While many Rush fans regard Peart as one of the all-time great lyricists, a great number regard his lyrics as verbose and pretentious. Since his fantastical swords-and-sorcery lyrics that began in earnest on *Caress of Steel* to the widely criticised 'Tai Shan' and beyond, there is probably no Rush lyric that has been more criticised than 'Dog Years'.

Written early in the album's writing sessions while Peart was hungover, the song does contain, despite its critics, a few particularly pleasing lines; the most notable of which is a pun that is only available to those who read the lyric sheet and have some knowledge of ancient Greece: 'In the dog days/People look to Sirius'.

While a listener may initially hear Lee singing the word 'serious', Sirius is, in fact, also known as the 'Dog Star'. The ancient Greeks, who saw this particularly bright star shining during the day, attributed hot days (known as dog days) to the extra light it provided in daytime. Peart also indulges in an act of self reference—back to the *Signals* album: 'One sniff at the hydrant/And the answer is automatic'.

Regardless of the lyric, 'Dog Years' is Rush at their heavy best and is a joyful and puerile addition to the album.

'Virtuality'

Opening with what is surely one of Lifeson's most spectacular riffs, 'Virtuality' is an upbeat ode to the internet of 1996. Peart's decision to write about a technology that was, in many respects, in its infancy, inevitably doomed the song to date extremely quickly. Nevertheless, it is something of a time capsule. Lifeson's discordant harmonics during the pre-chorus are designed to mimic the dial-up tone of an old style modem.

Although the song's lyric has met criticism from those that see it as a little too hackneyed, the song is a genuine expression of interest in what is unquestionably one of the great technological advances of humankind. The line 'I can save the universe/In a grain of sand' is a fine example of Peart's use of poetic imagery to speak fact, since almost limitless information is indeed stored on silicon chips.

The simple bones of the song are fleshed out with intricate textural layers and a memorable melody, which make the song a strong point of the album, despite the fact that it is unlikely to be noted by many Rush fans as a favourite.

'Resist'

Originally titled 'Taboo' to reference Freud's book *Totem and Taboo*, the band eventually decided to opt for its simpler final title. Riffing on one of Oscar Wilde's most famous quotes, 'I can learn to resist anything but temptation', the lyric urges one to feed one's virtues and overcome one's failures. The entire lyric can be summed up in its final lines: 'You can fight … without ever winning/But never ever win … without a fight'.

Lee often introduced the song (after adopting a Scottish accent) as 'inspired by the great country of Scotland', Lifeson incorporates some of the Celtic-inspired melodies he had become enamoured with into the piece, foregoing a traditional solo and instead including a slow and soaring melodic guitar line.

'Limbo'

With its title a pun on the right-wing talk show host Rush Limbaugh, this strange instrumental is a patchwork of whirling textures, tumbling fills, and surreal rock.

Before working on the song, Peart had been trying to remember the lyrics to the 1962 novelty hit 'Monster Mash', which led to several samples from the track being included on 'Limbo', as Peart explains:

> … our co-producer, Peter Collins, went out and bought a CD that had a compilation of some funny songs like that. We got to listening to it, thinking about how funny it

was and decided to put some samples of it in there. That's Igor going 'Goo mash goo.' We had to get special permission and pay money and everything. You think it's so strange, when you just want to make a joke, and people want you to get permission and pay money.[2]

'Carve Away the Stone'
Once again revealing Peart's interest in mythology, 'Carve Away the Stone' refers to the ancient myth of Sisyphus—the king who was punished by the gods for his arrogance. His eternal torment was to spend every day rolling a stone to the top of a hill only to watch it roll back to its starting place at the day's end. Peart uses this imagery as a metaphor for our own troubles and guilt, suggesting that if we must roll the stone, we could at least try to make it easier on ourselves and gradually 'chip away' at it. Peart's lyric makes the point that it is much easier to offer advice than take it—the entire song is a plea to a friend to chip and carve away at their stone, until the last line: 'If you could just move yours/I could get working on my own'.

With the track's slow tempo and grungy opening, it may initially appear an odd choice for the album's finale; however, with its subtle use of odd time signatures in the chorus as well as the song's sprightly bridge section, this song does have its merits, despite being largely forgotten within Rush's enormous repertoire.

Interesting Liner Notes
The album's cover features an Inukashuk—an Inuit signpost that indicates a high point of land in order to assist with navigation or hunting. Peart came upon one of these creations while hiking in Yellowknife and remarked that although in coming across it, he had not made contact with another person, he had experienced their echo.[3] It was for this reason he suggested using the impressive Inukashuk image on the front of the album. The album's back cover features a superimposed photograph of some of the SETI radio transceivers, which patiently await the return echo from extra-terrestrial life. Another of Syme's brilliantly thought out covers to feature a pleasing, yet congruent contrast.

Syme's work continues throughout the booklet with relevant original art alongside each lyric, as well as the addition of a still from the film *2001: A Space Odyssey* to accompany the lyric to 'Totem'. The liner notes, as always, do contain photographs of the band; though the ones included in this booklet are of Rush as youngsters.

Acknowledged for their 'friendly help and helpful friendship' are, among others, Primus, haggis, Martian Dweller (who provided the Dulcimer that is played at the beginning of 'Resist'), and, as always, 'last but far from least—our families'.

The album is brought to you by the letter 'R-r-r-r'.

17

Vapor Trails

Release date: 14 May 2002
Current edition: Atlantic CD
Recorded at Reaction Studios, Toronto
Produced by Rush and Paul Northfield
Recorded by Paul Northfield, Geddy Lee, and Alex Lifeson
Mixed by David Leonard
Chart position: Canada: 3
UK: 11
US: 6

Released in 2002, nearly six years after their last studio album, *Vapor Trails* is an unusual but vital part of Rush's career. With the band tentatively agreeing to work on the new album after a lengthy hiatus, *Vapor Trails*' long gestation began slowly. Peart's lack of enthusiasm for many of his previous passions had led him to give up drumming entirely for over two years, and thus, when he anxiously suggested that he may want to consider working with the band again, his friends and colleagues, Lee and Lifeson, were sensitive to the fact that this album's production period would need to be less intense than their sixteen previous efforts. For this reason, the band, for the first time, agreed to work with absolutely no time constraints and no deadlines: the album would be finished when the band felt it was ready.

While Peart continued to work himself back into shape as a drummer, as well as penning several heartfelt lyrics, Lee and Lifeson recorded hours of jam sessions. These recordings were then pored over by Lee, finding parts that he believed may become the constituents of a song. These individual parts were then digitally pieced together, a guide drum part was added, and the completed songs were then sent to Peart. This lengthy and arguably inorganic process took an enormous amount of time.

Production duties were taken on by Paul Northfield who had engineered several of the band's previous albums but had not produced them before.

Northfield once recalled how during the sessions for *Vapor Trails*, the band considerably altered what had been an unsuitable and under-equipped studio in order that they could complete the album at a location close to home.

Regardless of its quality, *Vapor Trails* was the album the band had to make in order to get back together and learn to function as Rush again. The album is the first of Rush's studio efforts to entirely forego the use of synthesizers since 1975's *Caress of Steel*. Lee and Lifeson decided instead to use multiple overdubs of heavily effect-driven guitar, bass, and vocals to thicken and layer the sound. This decision, as well as the decision to use many of the original jammed recordings, led the album's production to suffer enormously. The final mastering of the album was also extremely loud, leading to digital distortion. The band were ultimately unsatisfied with the album's production, as Lifeson explains:

> From the heavy stuff to the more melodic stuff, it was a very fragile representation of the band, in the way it was recorded. In mastering, unfortunately, it was a contest, and it was mastered too high, and it crackles, and it spits, and it just crushes everything. All the dynamics get lost, especially anything that had an acoustic guitar in it.[1]

Despite the album's production, it is an unquestionably passionate and fiery expression of the band at their most fragile. *Vapor Trails* is an album that many never believed would come to exist, and in many ways, ought to be regarded as Rush's second debut album.

Vapor Trails received mixed reviews upon release, and enjoyed moderate commercial success—it was the third highest charting album in Canada during 2002. The album's production was heavily criticised, and the entire lack of guitar solos was met with disappointment by many fans. However, *Vapor Trails* was an entirely unconventional album. It was recorded in circumstances that very few bands would ever find themselves in and ultimately it was an experiment in working together again; an experiment that would yield great success for the band for years to come.

While the album was heavily criticised for various reasons, the lyrics were praised for their depth of heart, and particularly noted by Rush fans as being deeply personal in comparison to most of Peart's previous work. In years to come, many fans would grow to appreciate the songs on *Vapor Trails*, and after considerable pressure (not least from themselves), the band would eventually have the entire album remixed in order to help fix many of the production issues.

Songs

'One Little Victory'
With a burst of blasting bass drums, a pulsing hi-hat, and the multiplying cracks of Peart's snare, 'One Little Victory' explodes into life with a proud and

disobedient intensity. Peart's opening statement on the album immediately silences the doubters—he is back; Rush are back.

The lyric speaks of defiance in the face of defeat and a determination to continue to pursue victory—such perfect correlation between music and lyric is rare in any music, but is found here. It is clear why the band had no doubt that the album should open with this explosive track.

'Ceiling Unlimited'

Yet another of Peart's lyrics that highlights his enthusiasm for weather. 'Ceiling Unlimited' is a term applied to a cloudless (or nearly cloudless) sky. The song uses this imagery as a metaphor for the enormity of the world, full of such wonder that is so often ignored.

Despite the brick-walled production, 'Ceiling Unlimited' features some of the album's rare moments of musical dynamics with some intelligent rhythmic interplay.

The line 'If culture is the curse of the thinking class' is a response to Oscar Wilde's famous adage 'Drink is the curse of the working class'—the lyric's criticism is extended to all.

Despite the song's initial cynicism, it is ultimately hopeful, concluding with Lee's soaring refrain 'Hope is like an endless river/The time is now again'. This imagery was used by Peart as a response to Thomas Wolfe's book *Of Time and the River*.

'Ghost Rider'

Thematically and musically the album's linchpin, 'Ghost Rider' amazingly almost failed to make the album's final cut. With such a deeply personal and expository lyric, it was vital that the band found the right tone for the song. Thankfully, Northfield, in his role as producer, was able to suggest changes to the song's arrangement, which the band found agreeable, and so the song survived.

The lyric, which is the core of the song, began life during Peart's 55,000-mile motorbike journey; during which he travelled across Canada to Alaska then south through the United States and Mexico until reaching Belize. Peart's journey was a direct response to the bereavements he had experienced only a short while prior. Much of the lyric was initially part of a song called 'Telescope Peak', which Peart wrote after climbing this, the highest point in the Death Valley National Park. According to Peart, the 'best lines' of this lyric were then used to create the lyrics for 'Ghost Rider' and 'How It Is'.

The song's title existed long before the song itself. On his travels, Peart took a series of themed photographs of his motorbike apparently travelling with no rider. These 'Ghost Rider' photos would be published inside Peart's book of the same name, and were also displayed as projections while the band performed the song live.

'Peaceable Kingdom'

While many bands attempt to give a sense of spontaneity in their studio recordings, few achieve it. In 'Peaceable Kingdom', however, the listener is quite genuinely hearing the song being played for the first time. Much of the song was taken from Lee and Lifeson's extended jam sessions. Using computer technology to stitch together and repeat the best parts, the bones of the song were completed. The drums and additional overdubs were added later, but nevertheless, the track is a true example of spontaneous composition released as a final product.

The song's title refers to a series of paintings of the same name, each depicting the words of Isaiah 11:6–8. Contained in this Bible verse is the famous imagery of the lion and ox living together in peace.

Peart's exasperated lyric questions how humanity with all its differences of opinion and understanding can ever reconcile itself in this way. For all the pursuit of truth and light, there will always be those who, in pursuing their own self-righteous path, bring death and destruction.

The tarot card imagery that is printed alongside each of the song's lyrics inside the album inlay depicts The Tower card: a blazing tower from which its burning occupiers jump. The reference to the, still relatively recent, attacks on the World Trade Center in New York are plain to see.

'The Stars Look Down'

Just over a decade earlier in *Roll the Bones*, Peart made the case for his worldview: our fortunes play a role in our lives, but ultimately, with hard work and persistence, we can load the dice, improve our odds, and change our fate. 'The Stars Look Down' takes a far more jaded and even fatalistic view of the same subject. We may feel we are in control, but ultimately our lives are entirely at the mercy of fate.

While Peart had often used his lyrics to promote the heroic side of humanity, the use of flies and rats as metaphors for everyday people cuts to the core of Peart's quite understandable internal torment. The 'fly on the wheel' is a reference to the Aesop's fable *The Fly and the Draught-Mule*.

While the song's music swells and recedes, leaving a good deal more space than much of the album's other material, the lighter areas of the song do highlight the loud, compressed, and distorted production that blights the entire album. Nevertheless, the song's lush arrangements do shine through at certain moments. The song's instrumental segment, for instance, switches between cacophonous noise and layers of ambient guitars giving the listener some rare light and shade on this otherwise relentless album.

The song's title was taken from the book of the same name by A. J. Cronin. At the time of writing, Peart had not read the book, but felt enthused by the title and its description of an amoral universe.

'How It Is'

Lifeson's jangling twelve-string guitar gives this sometimes folky song an unusual quality, particularly for a Rush song. Switching between a rapid, gravelly hard rock verse, and a melodic and spacious chorus, it is a fine musical representation of its lyric.

While the song displays to the listener clear audible contrast, the lyric speaks of the contrast of one's present situation and the potential future: 'How it is and how it ought to be'. In our darkest moments, our minds sometimes trick us into believing that the difficulties we are experiencing are insurmountable—the world is fixed as it is and good days are consigned to the past.

While the song, with its dark imagery, may initially appear to be a simple observation of the world's ills, it is, in fact, another of Peart's lyrical kicks of encouragement: accepting that things are as bad as they seem, and yet reminding the listener that things will improve—the clouds will pass. The song, however, does not simply urge for the passage of time to move the clouds along. The lines of encouragement at the end of the song are taken from Thomas Wolfe: 'Foot upon the stair/Shoulder to the wheel'.

The line 'You can't tell yourself how to feel' is something of a mini-motto that Peart adopted while on his Odyssean motorcycle journey.

'Vapor Trail'

In stark contrast to the tentatively optimistic 'How It Is', 'Vapor Trail' is as unflinchingly bleak as a song can be. Like the trails of thick condensation left in the wake of a soaring aircraft, our lives are full of energy and substance, but ultimately, like the vapour trail itself, we disappear, leaving no trace of our existence. Unlike many of Peart's lyrics (including many on this very album), 'Vapor Trail' offers no caveats to this dark world-view. Peart's attitude seems to be: this is it, we must deal with it.

Largely inspired by W. H. Auden's famous 'Funeral Blues'. The despair and hopelessness after a bereavement were captured by Auden with his lines: 'Pour away the ocean and sweep up the wood/For nothing now can ever come to any good'. Peart paraphrases these lines as well as riffing further on Auden's desire to 'pack up' and 'dismantle' the universe itself.

After seeing the lyric, Lee found it extraordinarily difficult to find the proper musical approach to these deeply heartfelt lyrics. Eventually, after almost giving up on the task, he took three simple chords that, without conscious thought, invited a melody that seemed perfectly appropriate; thus, the song was composed.

Another difficulty the band had was deciding on a name for the album. Ultimately, they took the decision to refer to the album in the most fatalistic of ways, referring to each of the new songs as a transient vapour trail.

'Secret Touch'

Lee's favourite track on the album, 'Secret Touch', once again switches between laid-back ambient textures and storming heavy rock. Peart once again uses lines from books that had sustained him on his enormous motorcycle journey: Chitra Banerjee Divakaruni's *Sister of My Heart* gives us the line 'There is never love without pain', while Joseph Conrad's *Victory* gives us the song's title within the line 'A secret touch on the heart'.

This 'secret touch' refers to the subtle ways that a few important people were able to truly comfort and console Peart during his heartbroken and grief-ridden days immediately after his bereavements. While the main part of the lyric describes the sense of depersonalisation and isolation that is so often experienced by the bereaved, these 'healing hand(s)' offered a thread linking Peart to the rest of the world.

The final part of the song is an extended jam with some fantastically nuanced drumming. In the live setting, the band would use this free and open arrangement to great effect. The lyric concludes defiantly: 'Life is the power that remains'.

'Earthshine'

The first song to be completed during the *Vapor Trails*' sessions, this heavy and evocative piece was tinkered with and altered until it was, eventually, entirely rewritten into its final form.

Peart uses the lyric to describe an astronomical phenomenon, known as earthshine. As Peart's lyrics explain: 'On certain nights/When the angles are right/And the moon is a slender crescent' the sun's light, reflected by the earth, gives a soft illumination to what would have been the dark portion of the moon.

Aside from the beauty of the phenomenon itself, the lyric briefly touches on earthshine as a metaphor: 'Pale facsimile/Like what others see/When they look in my direction'. Like the ghostly moon, our outward appearance only gives a vague impression of who we really are.

The final verse edges into the realms of an extraordinarily subtle love song. The narrator regards themselves as the moon, whose face, illuminated by the sun (by 'third-hand' light), glorifies the star, without whom there would be no light at all. Despite the beauty of the ghostly moon, it is the modest and unseen sun that provides the beauty. The moon relies on the sun for illumination as the narrator relies on others for inspiration.

'Sweet Miracle'

A more traditional arrangement with minimal overdubs makes 'Sweet Miracle' reminiscent of the traditional power-trio work Rush had been known for on previous albums. Lee's chordal bass work coupled with Peart's expressive drumming give an entertaining foundation to a simple, memorable melody.

The lyric describes despair, anger, and ultimately transcendence. From the depths of pain, love can bring us back to life. Another autobiographical work from Peart, a style of writing that until *Vapor Trails* had been extremely rare for him.

'Nocturne'

While the subject of dreams is a common theme throughout Rush's repertoire, the literal nightly dreams we all experience had rarely, if ever, been touched on. Peart was inspired to write the lyric after reading a magazine article about a man who decided to seek medical advice after a series of premonitory nightmares. Convinced by these vivid dreams that something was seriously wrong with his body, a doctor confirmed that a cancerous tumour was growing on his thyroid. Continuing to monitor his dreams, he heard a recurring phrase while asleep: 'You have been living on the outer shell of your being; the way out is the way in!' part of which was used in the song 'Secret Touch'.[2]

After a short break in the writing process, Lee and Lifeson embarked on a writing period that Lee describes as the 'best jams Alex and I have ever had'.[3] Out of these sessions came 'One Little Victory', 'Ceiling Unlimited', and 'Nocturne'. Peart remarked in the *Vapor Trails*' tour book that the song's more experimental arrangements are a result of a growing confidence between the members of the band in the writing process gained after several months of working together again.

'Nocturne' is a good example of Lee's decision, after eschewing keyboards, to use his voice a textural instrument. Layers of effect-laden vocal fill the arrangement and colour it to a great degree.

'Freeze (Part IV of "Fear")'

With its odd time signature and harsh rhythmic guitar, 'Freeze' brings to mind the heart-pounding confusion of fright. While the 'Fear' series was initially planned as a trilogy, nearly two decades after its supposed completion, 'Freeze' was added to create the tetralogy. The song discusses the physical reaction to fear and the so called 'fight-or-flight' response. Many animals do not act in either fashion and freeze, sometimes playing dead, sometimes stunned by an overwhelming situation.

Lifeson's unconventional creativity comes to the fore throughout this song, during which he layers the song with a mixture of heavy rhythmic jabs, growling rhythmic guitar, and the light jangling tones of acoustic guitars.

'Out of the Cradle'

With its title taken from Walt Whitman's poem 'Out of the Cradle Endlessly Rocking', this hopeful piece ends the album with the same defiance that 'One Little Victory' opened it with. Full of triumphant optimism, Lee's vocal performance is arguably made more powerful by the despair and sorrow that has occupied much of the preceding album. Peart's lyric is joyous: 'Surge of energy, spark of inspiration/The breath of love is electricity'.

The song's explosive energy is relentless, and as the band begin to jam during the song's outro, many familiar Rush sounds return: Lifeson's incendiary chords, Lee's hyperactive flamenco bass, and Peart's wild Keith Moon-esque fills. If there was any doubt that Rush had returned in full force, the song's final statement, 'Here we come out of the cradle/Endlessly rocking', made the band's intentions clear.

Interesting Liner Notes

Hugh Syme's painting of an unstoppable fireball, leaving a faint vapour trail behind it, creates another powerful cover.

As well as Syme's portraits of the band, the inlay features imagery of tarot cards alongside each song. Peart had become somewhat interested in this form of divination while travelling through the USA, and thus, the imagery made its way into the album artwork.

The booklet features a somewhat enigmatic message in its final page:

> As always, we owe our families a huge debt
> of love, gratitude, appreciation, and attention
> We also owe them an apology.
> The album is 'Brought to you by the letter "3"'.

Vapor Trails Remixed

Released: 27 September 2013
Current edition: Rhino CD
Mixed by David Bottrill
Chart positions: Canada: 24
UK: 54
US: 35

After the release of 2002's *Vapor Trails*, despite the thrill of having Rush back as a recording entity, virtually everyone who heard it criticised the album's muddy, loud, and undefined sound quality. While the band remained tight lipped about their feelings, eventually they would come to reveal that they too had their own misgivings about the album's sound.

Lee would often drolly refer to the mixing process as 'the death of hope', and in the extended and stressful *Vapor Trails'* sessions, this already taxing period became impossibly difficult. Lee later revealed:

> *Vapor Trails* was an album made under difficult and emotional circumstances—sort of like Rush learning how to be Rush again—and as a result, mistakes were made that we have longed to correct. David Bottrill's remixes have finally brought some justice and clarity to this deserving body of our work.[4]

This thorough remix breathes life into an album that was, for many, difficult to listen to. The previously crowded sonic landscape has been carefully thinned. Brilliant musical flourishes that were inaudible on the first release now have their rightful place at the fore of this album. At last, this unique set of Rush songs could receive their due appreciation.

Snakes and Arrows

Release date: 1 May 2007
Current edition: Atlantic CD
Strings on 'Faithless': Ben Mink
Recorded at Allaire Studios, Shokan
Additional recording at Grandmaster Recorders, Hollywood
Produced by Rush and Nick Raskulinecz
Engineered by Richard Chycki
Mixed by Richard Chycki
Chart positions: Canada: 3
UK: 13
US: 3

During the mid-1970s, Rush's work pace was so intense that between performing and recording, there was little, if any, downtime to allow for writing. Consequently, the vast majority of songs were written in hotel rooms and tour buses, with Lee and Lifeson playing acoustic guitars. It is this back-to-basics approach that colours much of *Snakes and Arrows*.

Inspired by their work on *Feedback*, this new Rush album is a step forward by the band into new territory, but it nevertheless features clear influences from the psychedelic and blues rock that initially inspired the band back in the 1960s.

The album was produced by Nick Raskulinecz, who had made his name producing several Foo Fighters albums. This young and open-minded producer had grown up listening to Rush and was keen for the band to push themselves musically, encouraging the band to add more complexity and technicality to the music they were producing. Peart remarks that Nick would regularly state 'Hey, I wouldn't ask if I didn't know you could do it!'[1]

Lee would eventually rechristen Raskulinecz with the nickname 'Booujze'—a play on the producer's vocalisation of the bass drum and crash cymbal that ended so many of his suggested drum fills.

Inspired by the music Lee and Lifeson had produced in the early pre-production stages, Peart described the essence of the band's new material as 'spiritual'. Fans would later hear an album that was savagely critical of organised religion and drew inspiration from many of the modern 'free thinkers' and 'new atheists' of the early twenty-first century.

Coming immediately after Rush's covers album *Feedback* (see final chapter), *Snakes and Arrows* is at once a nostalgic and progressive release. With clear nods to the bands that influenced Rush in their very early days, the album is full of folky and at times psychedelically charged music. Nevertheless, the band's decision to hire a new producer coupled with their incessant drive to explore new sounds makes this album an interesting mix of old and new.

While the production does not have the clarity of some their earlier releases, and was still criticised by some for its loudness, *Snakes and Arrows* is a sea change from *Vapor Trails*, which so many regarded as unlistenable. Raskulinecz was able to provide the band with a modern rock production and yet was still, perhaps more so than any other Rush producer, able to have the band indulge in their own proud history.

So many Rush albums are clearly visible in retrospect as stepping stones and *Snakes and Arrows* is one of them. *Clockwork Angels*, the band's final album at the time of writing, would never have been possible without the groundwork established on *Snakes and Arrows*.

Songs

'Far Cry'

Imbued with the 'raw sophistication' that Peart claims colours much of the album, 'Far Cry' opens the album with a blast of twenty-first-century rock production, but with clear nods back to the band's earlier days: Lifeson's so called 'Hemisphere's chord' makes an appearance in the song just seconds after its beginning.[2]

'Far Cry' is an honest look at the world as it appears from Peart's perspective. His youthful optimism has given way to scepticism. The world, with its madness, anger, and repression, is 'A far cry from the world we thought we'd inherit'. Nevertheless, it allows us moments of beauty and truth, and with persistence, we can continue to enjoy these.

One of the later songs to be written for *Snakes and Arrows*, 'Far Cry' came together extraordinarily quickly. Lifeson explains that 'It was almost like we already knew the song when we wrote it. We just played it'.[3] Peart's lyrics had already been submitted and were met with enthusiastic approval. When Lee came to sing them over the new piece, they were a remarkable fit, and this relatively complex song was, in essence, completed in a fantastically short space of time.

'Armor and Sword'

A metaphor for faith, 'Armor and Sword' is Peart's comment on the positive and negative aspects of faith; on the one hand, it is a consolatory and reassuring protector, but it can quickly become a tool of aggression and dominance: 'Our suit of shining armor becomes a sharp and angry sword'.

Appropriately, the song is a musical expression of this duality. Pounding aggressive drums give way to lush, layered melodic guitars.

The line 'confused alarms of struggle and flight' was taken verbatim from the similarly themed poem 'Dover Beach' by Matthew Arnold.

'Workin' Them Angels'

'You workin' them angels overtime!' is a phrase Peart first overheard as a woman castigated her husband for his dangerous driving. Finding this phrase amusing, he adopted it himself. Peart has often spoken about the balance of risk and reward, particularly regarding many of his personal pursuits. Peart explains: '… a certain level of risk in life seemed worthwhile for the promised return—excitement and treasured experiences'.[4]

A relatively simple song, 'Workin' Them Angels' is, at its core, a folk song—as Lifeson's bouzouki interlude reveals. Nevertheless, Peart's strident drumming and Lee's bluesy vocal delivery give the song an interesting and unusual feel.

'The Larger Bowl'

'The Larger Bowl' is a title that had been percolating in Peart's brain since it came to him in a 'dysentery dream' during his 1988 cycle tour of West Africa. The lyric is in the form of a pantoum: a Malay verse structure in which the second and fourth line of each verse are used as the first and third of the next. This unusual form is initially jarring, but Lee's commitment to his vocal delivery gives the lyric a firm foundation and protects it from the dangers of apparent gimmickry.

Thematically, the song would not be out of place on *Vapor Trails* with its sorrowful regard of the stark inequality in the world. There is no uplifting caveat, only the bitter observation: 'Such a lot of pain on the earth'.

One of Rush's sparsest arrangements, 'The Larger Bowl' features lengthy periods of only vocal and guitar, while an upbeat folk-inspired chorus provides the basis for an angular and emotive guitar solo.

'Spindrift'

Featuring some of the heaviest work on the album, 'Spindrift' is another song of stark light and shade. Lifeson's guitar squeals and crashes like the tormented waves in the song's lyric when, with little warning, the storm abates and is replaced by light and transcendent textures.

The poet Robert Frost's epitaph 'I had a lover's quarrel with the world' influenced Peart to write this song. The exasperated, raging lyric 'What am

I supposed to do?/Where are the words to answer you?' are evocative of the personal and private stresses of life, and yet this song is truly global in its outlook. When this song was written, the world was fraught with conflict. With considerable Western intervention in the Middle East and the rise of religious terrorism, the world seemed locked in conflict: 'As the waves crash in/On the western shore/The wind blows fierce from the east'.

The phenomenon of spindrift itself is yet another example of Peart's encyclopaedic knowledge of weather. During a gale of Force 8 or above, the crests of waves will begin to break off in the wind direction into their own foamy white drifts. Watching for this is an indication for sailors that a gale is becoming particularly severe.

'The Main Monkey Business'

The final song to be recorded during the *Snakes and Arrows* sessions, 'The Main Monkey Business' was, at the behest of their new producer, recorded live in the studio with the intention of capturing the excitement and energy of the band as an interacting, improvising unit.

The band's previous instrumental, 'Limbo', released a decade earlier, shares many traits with this piece—with a focus on textures and soundscapes rather than pure instrumental wizardry. The numerous unexpected changes take the band firmly back into the realms of progressive rock.

In his essay, *The Game of Snakes and Arrows*, Peart reveals that this piece was unquestionably the hardest to write, arrange, and record among all of the album's other songs. It took him three days to learn the song's structure before any recording could begin.

The title of the piece comes from a conversation Lee had with his Polish mother about a relation; Peart recounts:

> She said, 'I have a feeling he's up to some monkey business.' Geddy laughed, saying, 'What kind of monkey business?' 'You know,' she said, with Old World wisdom, 'The main monkey business.' Everybody knows about that.

'The Way the Wind Blows'

More than thirty years after their debut, Rush were still incorporating new sounds into their music to surprise and delight their fans. This song's howling blues intro is almost unidentifiable as Rush; nevertheless, the upbeat hard rock groove that follows returns the band to familiar territory.

'The Way the Wind Blows' describes the balance required to be defiant in the face of oppression. Practically, we must adapt to our situation 'We can only bow to the here and now/Or be broken down blow by blow'. The song is savagely critical of organised religion, 'It's a plague that resists all science', and considers that the titular wind begins to bend and shape us from infancy, 'It seems to leave them partly blind/And they leave no child behind'.

Regularly introduced on the album's tour as one of the band's favourites, 'The Way the Wind Blows' is another genuine progression for the band. The lyric is an example of Peart at his incisive best.

'Hope'

The shortest Rush song on any album, 'Hope' is regarded by Peart as 'a kind of secular prayer'.[5] This short solo piece for twelve-string guitar was written by Lifeson and recorded in one take.

'Hope' is further evidence of Lifeson's enormous admiration for Jimmy Page, whose influence can be heard from the outset.

A live version of the song was nominated, but failed to receive, a Grammy award.

'Faithless'

While the narrator in 'The Way the Wind Blows' appears resigned to compliance with the stronger forces of nature in the world, 'Faithless' seems to be a quietly defiant companion piece: 'Like the willows in the wind/Or the cliffs along the ocean/I will quietly resist'—while a little bending, and a little crumbling may be inevitable, a stoic and dignified resistance can still be mounted.

This piece with its cathartic, anthemic chorus, swelling strings, and emotive Lifeson solo is something like a hymn for the unbeliever. With laser-guided precision, Peart targets the 'Fools and thieves' that are so dangerous as they occupy places of work and worship. Despite the deep criticism of religion that is evident in this song, it is ultimately a piece about autonomy, and self-determination: 'I still cling to hope/And I believe in love/And that's faith enough for me'.

'Bravest Face'

With its laid-back verses, 'Bravest Face' sounds like a response by the band to many of their early 1960s influences. Lifeson's solo is another surprising moment from a guitarist who had for so many years been pushing at the boundaries of the instrument's sound—a charmingly simple blues solo that gives way to a folky breakdown. The chorus, however—the lynchpin of the song—is typical Rush: powerful, rhythmically interesting, and coloured by Lifeson's subtle texturing.

In 'Bravest Face', Peart asks the listener to face up to the facts that life is not the songs or stories we hear, nor the programmes we watch on TV, life exists in reality. Living, as we do, in a world without magic, we must value the 'precious little' we have and face the world with our 'bravest face'.

'Good News First'

In its early form, 'Good News First' was another largely acoustic arrangement and was, at the time, regarded by Lifeson as one of the weaker tracks on the album. As this dissatisfaction grew, the band decided to totally rearrange the track and give it a heavier electrified sound. The song's melody was also arranged differently, with Lee's original vocal line being played by a Mellotron: an instrument that the band had not used since 1975's 'Tears'.

Peart's lyric once again uses the device found earlier on 'Spindrift'. The lyric presents what is apparently a quarrel between two people, but in fact represents Peart debating a huge group of people. 'Good News First' speaks of loss of faith in a 'Benevolent Universe', but also of the enduring nature of beauty. As in 'Bravest Face', this song suggests we must make the best of what we have, 'So never mind the bad news/Let's have the good news instead', or alternatively as Peart puts it: 'Give me the ice cream, then give me the medicine, not the other way around'.[6]

'Malignant Narcissism'

This short, punchy, instrumental owes its existence to Nick Raskulinecz. Lee had recently been sent a Jaco Pastorius signature jazz bass from Fender and was absentmindedly noodling in the studio when 'Boouzje' immediately began recording him through a vocal mic. After a small amount of persuasion, their new producer had the band agree to record a new piece for the album—a bass and drum extravaganza.

Trey Parker and Matt Stone are friends of Peart's and allowed the band to use a sample from their latest film *Team America: World Police* part way through this instrumental. A voice can be heard saying 'Usually a case of malignant narcissism is brought on during childhood', from which the title is taken. However, Peart has also noted that the title is appropriate for a piece that has both bass and drum solos.

Peart opted to record the song on a small four-piece drum set, 'just for fun'.[7]

'We Hold On'

Snakes and Arrows provides the listener with a detailed panorama of the many and varied difficulties we face as human beings. The final track of the album is a discussion on how so many of us respond to the problems we face: we hold on. Like the 'precious little' described in 'Bravest Face', we cling to what we have—perhaps out of habit rather than logic. Though we are 'tempted to cut and run', so many times we persist out of habit with our lives.

Once again referencing his literary heroes, Peart's line 'Straining against a fate/Measured out in coffee breaks' takes its influence from T. S. Eliot's *The Love Song of J. Alfred Prufrock*.

For a song that is essentially a resignation, the music is remarkably defiant: typically Rush in its driving chorus and exuberant instrumental section.

A nod to Rush's early years, the line 'Long to give up the same old way' is double tracked with an additional whispered vocal—identical to the technique used to give 1975's 'The Twilight Zone' its unsettling sound.

'We Hold On' finds Rush in fine musical form with frenetic guitar, and a tightly locked, explosive rhythm section. While not the most uplifting of lyrics to finish on, the music brings the album to its finale in spectacular style.

Interesting Liner Notes

The album's cover painting is a depiction of *The Leela of Self Knowledge*—the game that was also known as *Snakes and Arrows*.

Hugh Syme's images sit alongside each song lyric throughout the inlay while the rear image is remarkably similar to a photograph taken by Carrie Nuttall, Peart's second wife. The image can be seen on the cover of her book *Rhythm and Light*. Syme has reinterpreted the photograph as a painting and replaced Peart's drum sticks with a snake and arrow.

Lifeson gets his credit for 'Hope': 'composed and performed by Lerxst Lifeson, all by his own self'.

Lee thanks, among others, 'Duke and Ewan for their exceptional canine behaviour in a supporting role'. In his long list of thanks, Lifeson extends appreciation to Pink Floyd guitarist David Gilmour, who had been instrumental in encouraging Lifeson to write predominantly on acoustic guitar.

Peart thanks a typically large number of individuals, but 'at the heart of it all—Carrie'. The album is 'brought to you by the letter "sssss"'.

Clockwork Angels

Release date: 8 June 2012
Current edition: Roadrunner CD (UK)
Piano on 'The Garden': Jason Sniderman
String arranger: David Campbell
Recorded at Revolution Recording, Toronto and Blackbird Studios Nashville, Tennesse
Produced by Rush and Nick Raskulinecz
Engineered by Richard Chycki
Mixed by Nick Raskulinecz
Chart positions: Canada: 1
UK: 21
US: 2

Many casual Rush fans are surprised to discover that *Clockwork Angels* is in fact Rush's first and only true concept album. Telling the story of a small-town boy with big ideas who eventually heads out to make his mark on the wider world, it is easy to see the autobiographical nods to Peart's own life. Nevertheless, the fantasy 'steampunk' world that colours the story keeps the album firmly in the realms of fiction.

The album is as grand in narrative scope as it is in musical ideas. While *Snakes and Arrows* saw the band tentatively approaching some progressive sounds, *Clockwork Angels* sees the band throw caution to the wind with complicated and lengthy compositions that are full of the energy and on-the-edge playing that Rush were renowned for in their early days.

At the time, Peart declared that he intended the album to 'be my highest achievement lyrically and drumming wise'.[1] In order to achieve this, Peart was determined to add fluidity improvisation into his playing. Thus, rather than learning the pieces part by part, he would roughly familiarise himself with the song and be 'conducted' by returning producer Nick Raskulinecz in order that, while drumming, he could concentrate purely on the performance, rather than counting the bars and beats until a particular change.

The album was also notable for its considerable use of strings. Parts for six violins and two cellos were incorporated throughout the album.

As well as by the lyrics themselves, the album's story is told through short companion pieces that are found in the lyric sheet.

Clockwork Angels was released to almost universal acclaim, with fans praising the band for tapping into the complex, high-energy music that coloured much of their early work. The album is at once the band's most mature effort and also, arguably, one of their most fiercely energetic.

The album, unlike many concept albums, has little in the way of a continuing musical theme and would ('BU2B2' aside) arguably work as a collection of songs in any order. The story, like many legendary concept albums, has layers of meaning that grow and develop on repeated listens. Alongside the album itself, the story has been released as a novel and a graphic novel, both written by Kevin J. Anderson with the latter illustrated by Nick Robel.

Producer Raskulinecz was widely credited with encouraging the band to explore many of the high-energy 'old-Rush' sounds that made *Clockwork Angels* so loved, though he was criticised by some for the over-loud production and his encouragement of Lee to sing in a high register that many regard as now being beyond his reach.

Clockwork Angels, at the time of writing Rush's final album, is a genuinely progressive effort by a band who were breaking new ground even on their twentieth studio album. Released thirty-eight years after their debut, it may well document the proud end of an illustrious recording career.

Songs

'Caravan'

Along with its B-side 'BU2B', 'Caravan' was originally released as a single in 2010, two years before the release of the album *Clockwork Angels*. After returning from the successful *Time Machine* tour, the two songs were subtly remixed while work on the rest of the album began in earnest.

'Caravan' sees the album's protagonist looking back on the start of his life. A frustrated young man desperate, like Peart was, to break away from the apparently idyllic life on the farm where he grew up. At last, he starts his journey—an escape from the quiet life into the city. 'In a world where I feel so small/I can't stop thinking big'.

'BU2B'

Originally titled 'Brought up to Believe', this song's title was shortened by the band for ease of communication, and the shorter title stuck.

Differing from its single version only with a short acoustic introduction, 'BU2B' is a stridently heavy rock song with a furious, sarcastic lyric. Continuing many of the themes discussed on *Snakes and Arrows*, this song describes the way that beliefs that are introduced to children at a young age insidiously become a part of that person forever. The 'Loving Watchmaker' refers to the Big Brother-style leader who is, in this story, responsible for every aspect of life in the *Clockwork Angels* universe. The title is perhaps a reference to the 'Watchmaker Analogy'—an argument that posits that the universe must have been created by intelligent design, for without a mind behind it, the argument asks, how could the universe (like a watch) be so finely constructed within such infinitely small tolerances? Peart describes the song as 'faith-bashing'.

At this early point in the album's story, the protagonist begins to doubt that his fate is sealed—perhaps he can have more control over his life than he first thought.

The song's lyrics are peculiarly arranged, with the first half of the song using elements of the 'pantoum' form—the second line of each verse becomes the first of the next.

'Clockwork Angels'

The album's title track finds the story's hero in the heart of 'Crown City' with its immense Cathedral and, floating high above, the Clockwork Angels themselves—a world away from the idyllic farm from whence this young man came.

The people around gaze up in adoration for these beautiful, synthetic creations. The world is clockwork, not just in its rigid conformity, but also in its lack of humanity. The population of Crown City are captivated, mesmerised, and ultimately ruled by nothing more than technology. Nevertheless, the story's protagonist is overwhelmed by the incredible sight.

With huge suspended chords and chorus-laden arpeggios, 'Clockwork Angels' finds Lifeson sounding more like his typical self than he has for years. Lee and Lifeson have together created a soundtrack to Peart's cinematic lyric that adds colour and contrast to an already vivid scene.

'Clockwork Angels' finds Peart once again borrowing from a famous literary work: 'Lean not upon your own understanding'. The angels' command to faith borrowed from Proverbs 3:5.

'The Anarchist'

With its furious and unruly instrumentation, this song takes us inside the mind of The Anarchist, a malevolent character who represents the antithesis of the stiflingly precise Watchmaker. A wandering pedlar asks 'What do you lack?' The Anarchist sneers: 'Ah … vengeance'. Full of hatred and envy after a lifetime of pain, The Anarchist finds himself determined to exact revenge on those who are happier and more successful than he.

Lee decided to give The Anarchist an 'eight-string bass vibe' by multi-tracking two basses an octave apart. This offered more flexibility to control the tonality post-recording rather than just using a single eight-string instrument.

'The Anarchist' finds Rush utterly unrestrained in a way that they have not chosen to be for many years. Producer Nick Raskulinecz has a particular affection for this song as he describes:

> To me, it's all about the riff, and this riff takes me back to the old days. That was one of the cool things about working on this record, helping Rush to know that it was OK to be like this. 'You guys can do this. You guys did it a long time ago, you can do it again. You own it!' ... Vocally, it was about getting Geddy up in that high register where he belongs. His energy level is pretty cool here.[2]

'Carnies'

Returning to the story's hero, we find him having found work in a travelling carnival. The music is redolent of the intense lifestyle of the travelling performer. Heavy riffs and unusual tonality, coupled with another cinematic lyric, bring to mind the sights, sounds, and smells of this 'Steampunk' fayre: 'The glint of iron wheels.... The smell of flint and steel'.

In the second half of the song, 'a face of naked evil' appears: The Anarchist. He throws a time bomb towards the protagonist, who automatically catches it. His friends and colleagues turn to see him holding the bomb and assume the worst. Escaping with his body intact, but his life in ruins, our hero now finds himself utterly alone in the world.

Despite the intense and unruly music, 'Carnies' successfully melds heavy hard rock with memorable and emotive melodies—something of a coming together of early and modern Rush music.

'Halo Effect'

The 'halo effect' is a psychological phenomenon where confirmation bias leads us to make illogical judgements about a person—believing them to be who we would like them to be, rather than who they actually are. This song is about exactly that. The protagonist had, before his exile, fallen in love with one of the carnival performers: 'All my illusions/Projected on her/The ideal, that I wanted to see'.

Musically, 'Halo Effect' has the band take a step back from the burning intensity of the album so far. A slow-tempo arena-rocker, 'Halo Effect' is a short and laid-back display of songwriting maturity and closes the album's first half.

'Seven Cities of Gold'

Broken-hearted, lost, alone, and with nothing to lose, our protagonist crosses the Western sea for 'Poseidon, a tough port city'. Here he worked for a time before setting out to the Redrock Desert in search for Cibola: the most famous of the 'Seven Cities of Gold'.

Peart claims that Cormac McCarthy, author of *No Country for Old Men*, was a big influence on the ideas for this song.[3] In reality, the 'Seven Cities of Gold', while never found, were genuinely believed to exist in the region of what is now New Mexico. While in the process of conquering the New World, some explorers even claimed to have seen the cities, though were unable to reach them. Nevertheless, exploration parties, especially of Spanish conquistadors, were repeatedly sent in search of the elusive cities.

With its funky feedback soaked intro, 'Seven Cities of Gold' quickly develops into a '60s-style British Invasion riff-vehicle. The addition of a howling organ and driving, time-shifting chorus lift the song to further heights—Lee's vocals wailing in their upper register, reminiscent of Rush's earliest releases.

With winter setting in and close to death, our story's hero begins to accept that if the cities exist at all, he will never discover them.

'The Wreckers'

While Rush had always found ways of incorporating sounds associated with their influences into their own music, 'The Wreckers' opens with a riff that is so utterly like The Who it is almost jarring. This blast of energy may fool the listener into thinking things are getting better for our unfortunate hero; however, further tragedy awaits.

After admitting defeat in his quest to find the golden Cibola, the protagonist heads back to the city of Poseidon by boat. The ship is caught up in a disastrous storm and, just when hope seems lost, a signal light is seen, drawing the ship towards the supposedly safe harbour. However, the light was placed in order to draw the ship towards rocky terrain, where it would be wrecked and its cargo plundered. The crew and passengers were left to the icy waves and ultimately the nameless young man at the heart of this story is the only survivor.

This horrendous tale is made more-so by its basis in fact. Years ago, groups of 'wreckers' would commit this terrible crime off the coast of Cornwall. Peart became aware of this practice after its inclusion in Daphne du Maurier's *Jamaica Inn*.

If listeners find that 'The Wreckers' has a peculiarly different sound to other Rush songs, the reason is that its writing process was an unusual one. During its writing process, Lee and Lifeson swapped instruments, with Lee composing the jagged rhythm guitar while Lifeson added the smooth, gliding bass. Ultimately, they would revert to their native instruments for the recording, but the composition remained largely unchanged. The pair remarked that in swapping instruments, they became The Barenaked Ladies.[4]

'Headlong Flight'

'Headlong Flight' steps back from the album's story and sees the storyteller as he is now: in the twilight of his life. Despite all he has endured and the suffering that accompanied many of his adventures, the song's refrain is at its core: 'I wish that I could live it all again!' Incidentally, this line was taken from a conversation that Peart had with his late drum tutor, Freddie Gruber, who had the same wish. Peart, however, has the opposite attitude: 'That is not a feeling I have ever shared about the past. I remain glad that I don't have to do it all again'.[5]

Musically, 'Headlong Flight' is perhaps the most energetic, frenetic piece of music on the album. Deliberately referencing the effervescent 'Bastille Day', the piece is somehow deeply nostalgic but entirely immediate. Lee, Lifeson, and Peart each have moments to shine in this lengthy piece, which features individual drum, bass, and guitar solos in addition to its always extravagant instrumentation.

'BU2B2'

A stark return to the story itself, our protagonist finds himself in the depths of despair. The beliefs that were at once so close to him have failed him at last: 'Life goes from bad to worse/No philosophy consoles me/In a clockwork universe'. Despite the pain of grief, the protagonist is still able to find 'A measure of love and laughter/And another measure to give'.

The meaning that life once had has gone entirely, but now occupying that space is a belief in the value of love and life itself.

The band struggled to incorporate 'BU2B2' into the album, but Peart, convinced it was a vital part, was determined to fit it in. Eventually, the guitars that accompanied Lee's vocals were replaced with a drone of cellos and synthesizers, leaving us with the vaguely Eleanor Rigby-esque track that made it on to the album.

This piece at only one minute and thirty seconds is less a song and more a segue into the album's final section: a summary of the story so far, and a quiet contrast to the blast of 'Wish Them Well' that follows.

'Wish Them Well'

Referred to by Peart as the 'trouble child' of the album, the finished song is in fact the third iteration of the piece. The two prior attempts were entirely abandoned. Even when the structure of the song was finally finished, the vocals and drums were altered innumerable times before the band were satisfied with the final product. Ironically, despite its teething troubles, 'Wish Them Well' is one of the simplest tracks on the album, with a straight-forward chord progression, no time changes, and, by Rush's standards, little musical intricacy.

'Wish Them Well' finds the story of *Clockwork Angels* coming to its end. The character has been exiled, broken-hearted, bereaved, and has lost everything, except his strength of character. Refusing to be defined by his pain, or by those who would hurt him, he wishes them well and departs. There is no forgiveness for those who have hurt him, though neither is there anger—only indifference.

One of Peart's constant lyrical themes of persistence is distilled into one line towards the end of 'Wish Them Well': 'Even though you're going through hell/ Just keep on going'.

Lifeson credits the band's long-serving engineer Rich Chycki for the 'huge and classic ... sick Marshall sound' that gives the song much of its power.[6] Strident Townshend-style rhythm guitar is once again used to great effect on this, the album's penultimate song.[7]

'The Garden'

In the short text that accompanies the lyric to 'The Garden' inside the album's booklet, Peart credits one of the main inspirations for the *Clockwork Angels'* story: Voltaire's *Candide*. After a life of struggle and misadventure, not dissimilar to the one experienced by Peart's character, *Candide* states that even after a life of struggle we must continue to 'tend our garden'. Peart's lyric is ultimately a piece about what he believes are life's most important aspects: love and respect.

Regarded by Lee as one of his proudest moments as a songwriter, 'The Garden' through its many subtle changes remains led by its gentle melody and heartfelt vocal. The addition of David Campbell's strings adds another layer to the track. Peart reveals that, upon first hearing the song with the overlaid strings, nobody in the studio was dry-eyed.[8]

Lifeson's improvised solo was, like many others, initially recorded as a 'throwaway' solo to stand in place until the final contribution was ready to record; however, the quality of Lifeson's delicate, heartfelt solo was immediately seen and it remains unchanged on the album.

'The Garden' is a song about a life completed. While the character singing it is fictional, Peart's words have an added depth now that, at the time of writing, it would appear that 'The Garden' is Rush's swansong—their final stamp on the world of songwriting, the final statement from a band who, like their fans, have grown and changed in incredible and unexpected ways.

Interesting Liner Notes

Hugh Syme's brilliant artwork allows the listener to fully immerse themselves into the album's 'steampunk' world. With cogs, alchemic symbols, and images of the steam liners and ships that are central to the album's story filling the pages of the booklet, the depth of the album's concept is increased further still.

The album's cover itself features twelve alchemy runes, each referring to one of the album's twelve songs. Each alchemy rune is in the place of a number on a clock face. The cover's clock reads approximately 9.12—presumably in the evening.

Each of the band typically thank an enormous number of people. Geddy uses his thank you space to, among other things, 'introduce ... The Wassermans ^..^ ^..^'.

Peart offers his thanks to 'Brutus and Bubba's Bar 'n' Grill, Freddie Gruber RIP' and his wife and daughter: 'Lastest and mostest—Carrie and Olivia'

The album was recorded at Revolution Recording, Toronto, in October–December 2011, except for 'Caravan' and 'BU2B', which were recorded at Blackbird Studios, Nashville, in April 2010. The intro for the latter was recorded at Lifeson's home studio: 'Lerxst Mobile'.

Strings were arranged and conducted by David Campbell and piano on 'The Garden' was played by Jason Sniderman.

The album is 'brought to you by the letter "⚥"'—the alchemy symbol for amalgamation.

The band's portrait was taken by Andrew MacNaughtan, the band's long-serving photographer and friend. MacNaughtan died early in 2012 and the album is dedicated to his memory.

Live Albums, Solo Albums, and Curiosities

All the World's a Stage

Released: 29 September 1976
Current edition: Virgin/EMI CD
Recorded at Massey Hall, Toronto (11–13 June 1976)
Produced by Rush and Terry Brown
Engineered by Terry Brown
Chart positions: Canada: 6
UK: did not chart
US: 40

Around the world, major rock bands have always had their rites of passage. While American bands dream of playing Madison Square Garden and British bands dream of playing Wembley, the dream of most Canadian rockers has been, for many years, to perform at Toronto's Massey Hall. In 1976, Rush performed at this prized venue for three consecutive nights. The recordings made on these nights would be used to create the first official Rush live album.

Despite their disastrous prior tour, and buoyed by the impressive success of their latest album, *All the World's a Stage* records a moment in time of this unvanquished band—finally free from the shackles of a meddling record company and with a huge confidence in their repertoire.

Although this album was recorded over three nights, there are audible mistakes. Peart's snare drum is noticeably 'switched off' during part of 'The Temples of Syrinx', and there are numerous other small errors that the pernickety can (and do) pore over and criticise. Yet this album's strength lies not in its technical excellence (although the playing here generally transcends anything by contemporary rock bands of the time), this is an album that is excellent because it is a powerful, energetic, and faithful live album that captures the essence of Rush as they were 1976.

In the liner notes, the band state this:

> It is not perfect, but it is faithful to us and to you. We have tried to strike a careful balance between perfection and authenticity, and to create a finished work that you may enjoy, and we may be proud of.

New listeners to this album will notice its sheer relentlessness. The palpable power and energy is constant throughout. Even the lighter 'Lakeside Park' has a punch that is not found on the studio recording. Despite being introduced as a performance of 'side one from our latest album', the performance of '2112' has had its two slowest sections, 'Discovery' and 'Oracle: The Dream', excised. There is no respite; it is an album of unabated hard rock.

The final track on the album 'What You're Doing' was not available on the original CD release due to the time constraints of early CD technology. The vinyl and remastered CD, however, feature this incredible rendition of a song from the band's first album. Peart's drumming is thrillingly histrionic and infuses the song with a vitality that the studio version arguably lacked. At the end of the song, the crowd can be heard applauding for yet another encore and members of the band can be heard enthusiastically yelling 'wow, what a show—man, oh, man!' before a door can be heard slamming shut.

In the album's liner notes, the band go on to say that 'This album to us, signifies the end of the beginning, a milestone to mark the close of chapter one, in the annals of Rush'. Of their many guises, this album marks the end of Rush's period of being something close to a traditional hard rock band. It was after this album they would embark on their first major stylistic change since the introduction of Neil Peart to the band—the period that would go on to define them, some would say tarnish them, as a progressive rock band.

Exit...Stage Left

Released: 29 October 1981
Current edition: Virgin/EMI CD
Recorded at The Apollo, Glasgow, Scotland and The Forum, Montreal, Quebec
Produced by Terry Brown
Engineered by Paul Northfield
Chart positions: Canada: 7
UK: 6
US: 10

Five years and four studio albums after their debut live album, *All the World's a Stage*, Rush's second official live recording is remarkably different to its predecessor. While fans and critics had praised their first live effort for its raw power, Rush had made a conscious decision to make their second live album a more polished affair, to the extent that the performances were not just from different concerts but different tours. Sides 1, 3, and 4 of the double album were recorded at The Forum in Montreal while the band were touring their latest studio effort, *Moving Pictures*, and the performances on side 2 of the album were recorded at The Apollo in Glasgow while the band were on tour promoting *Permanent Waves*.

While the album has its moments of energetic brilliance, the band's enthusiasm to correct mistakes perhaps leads to a sterility in the performance, particularly in comparison to their previous live effort. Rush have always been early adopters of new technology, but their use of embryonic digital editing technology on *Exit... Stage Left* was perhaps to the album's detriment.

The album features several notable moments, however, not least an entirely new piece of music, 'Broon's Bane'. This extended classical introduction to 'The Trees', named in honour of the band's producer, would have been a pleasant surprise for fans of Lifeson's previously fleeting moments of classical guitar. 'Closer to the Heart' is invigorated by the lusty singing of the 'Glaswegian Chorus', who are thanked by the band in the album's liner notes: 'Nice one, folks!'

This album also features further evidence of Rush's unusual sense of humour. 'Jacob's Ladder' is introduced by Lee as a song that was 'done a long time ago by T. C. Broonsy' while the album's final track, 'La Villa Strangiato', features some peculiar vocals from Lee in the 'Danforth and Pape' section. The (loose) translation from the sung Yiddish is provided in the album's liner notes as follows: 'Patty-cake, patty cake/Mother's going to buy you shoes/Father's going to buy you socks/Baby's going to have red cheeks'.

The album's artwork is yet another impressive piece of work by Syme, who successfully incorporates motifs from each of the band's previous albums together on the front and rear of the album. The band had hoped to feature the absconding tail of the Hanna-Barbera feline, 'Snagglepuss', whose catchphrase was used as the title for the album. However, the band were unable to attain the right to do so.

While the album has gone down in Rush history as something of a classic, it is one of the few Rush albums that arguably, owing to its production process, has not stood the test of time. Terry Brown's strange mix leaves Lifeson's ordinarily fiery guitar to flounder in the background while some of the final tracks simply do not capture Rush's extraordinary live energy. This is an album with excellent material that is unfortunately let down by its production.

A Show of Hands

Release date: 9 January 1989
Current edition: Virgin/EMI CD
Recorded at Birmingham (UK) New Orleans, Phoenix, San Diego and Meadowlands, New Jersey (USA)
Produced by Rush
Engineered by Paul Northfield and Guy Charbonneau
Charted: Canada: did not chart
UK: 12
US: 21

Continuing the trend of releasing a live album after every fourth studio album, *A Show of Hands* was an attempt to find a happy medium between the rawness of *All the World's a Stage* and the sterility of *Exit...Stage Left*. The album begins with a quiet recording of the theme from *The Three Stooges*, which Rush were using as their intro music at the time. This disarming prelude suddenly gives way to a blistering performance of 'The Big Money', and after a matter of moments, it is clear that Rush have, at last, achieved their aim of a live album that captures the power and energy of their live shows without compromising on clarity of production.

Featuring performances from 1986's *Power Windows* tour as well as 1988's *Hold Your Fire* tour, the album is an impressive live catalogue of the band's recent repertoire—over half of the album is music from the band's two most recent studio albums.

As well as the brief nod to Cheech and Chong's 'Earache my Eye' at the end of 'The Big Money', the album contains another new piece: Peart's drum solo 'The Rhythm Method'. Like the rest of the album, it contains clear influences from work that was included on the band's previous live efforts, but has been updated with contemporary technology and synthesized to a large degree. Nevertheless, Peart still succeeds in recording a drum solo that is—at nearly five minutes long—still entertaining and at times melodic in its own right.

Lessons learnt after Terry Brown's ceaseless tinkering on *Exit...Stage Left* clearly had an impact on the band's decision to produce the album themselves. Ultimately, the listener is left with a powerful example of the band's live performances from the time.

Notably, 'Prime Mover', the song from which the album's title is taken, was not included on the audio release.

Different Stages

Released: 10 November 1998
Current edition: Virgin/EMI CD
Recorded at The World Amphitheater, Chicago; Spectrum, Philadelphia; Miami Arena; Starplex Amphitheater, Dallas; Great Woods Performing Arts Center, Mansfield, Massachusetts and (Disc 3) Hammersmith Odeon, London
Produced by Geddy Lee and Paul Northfield
Engineered by Paul Northfield
Hammesmith recording engineer: Terry Brown
Chart positions: Canada: 12
UK: 121
US: 35

Different Stages concludes the band's pattern of releasing a live album after every four studio albums. Traditionally, each live album had been a retrospective look at the material released over the band's recent career (with a few favourites in addition) but *Different Stages* was, tragically, quite different. The album has a short dedication inside its front cover: 'suddenly ... you were gone ... from all the lives you left your mark upon. In loving memory of Jackie and Selena'.

Shortly after finishing the *Test for Echo* tour, Peart had suffered two horrendous bereavements. The aftermath of these terrible events is detailed in his book, *Ghost Rider: Travels on the Healing Road.* In this book, he reveals that just before work had begun on *Different Stages*, he had asked his band mates to consider him retired. Understandably then, while Geddy Lee and producer Paul Northfield finished work on the album, they had good reason to believe that it would be the band's final release. Perhaps because of this, it was decided to include a third disc of music recorded at London's Hammersmith Odeon in 1978, as well as the recent live output (mainly recorded in Chicago in 1997). Thus, the album features an enormously diverse range of music from a large number of the band's albums.

While the production is not quite as polished as on their previous live album, *A Show of Hands*, *Different Stages* is an enormously powerful hard rock live album that exudes energy and effortlessly executed musical exuberance. The first two discs, which feature music from the band's *Test for Echo* and *Counterparts* tours demonstrate the band at the height of their powers and notably includes the only officially released complete live version of *2112*.

The album's third disc, while a welcome inclusion, is much more like 'bonus' material. The sound quality is, owing to recording techniques of the time, considerably poorer than the rest of the album and the band's hurriedly played early material, while impressively technical and youthfully ebullient, is notably less mature.

The album's visual design is another brilliant piece of work from Hugh Syme, made more effective by the considerable use of Andrew MacNaughtan's photographs. Given the retrospective nature of the album, the inlay features a chronological visual timeline of Rush paraphernalia: from photographs, tour books, and hand-written lyrics through to the eventual Gold Discs, awards, and backstage passes.

The simple artwork features three abacus beads, with one separated from the other two. This abstract art can easily be understood as relating to the album's three discs (with one considerably earlier than the other two), but its sad relevance as a visual metaphor of Peart's departure from the band is also clear.

Lee includes a short letter of thanks to all involved with the band's continued existence and success for the twenty-four years that had passed since the release of their first album. While it may have gone over the heads of many fans at the time, this appreciative letter was written by Lee in the knowledge that it may well have been the band's final statement.

Among the rest of the album's visual delights, it is easy to miss the photograph on the front of disc three. Featuring the Hammersmith Odeon as it was in 1978, there are two superimposed figures in the scene: a shady looking Lee is touting tickets on the left, while white-suited orderlies force Lifeson into an ambulance on the right.

Rush in Rio

Released: 21 October 2003
Current edition: Atlantic CD, Eagle Vision DVD/Blu-ray
Recorded at The Maracanã Stadium, Rio de Janeiro
Recorded by James 'Jimbo' Barton assisted by Patrick Thrasher
Assistant engineer: Kooster McAllister
Charted: Canada: n/a
UK: 139
US: 33

Recorded on the final night of the *Vapor Trails* tour, this live album features Rush performing to over 40,000 people, their second ever largest crowd: the largest was 60,000 the night before in São Paulo. The show in São Paulo had taken place outdoors under torrential rain and, aside from the band themselves being soaked, much of their equipment had stopped working as a result of the weather. The enormous clean-up at the end of the show coupled with travel problems meant that when the crew arrived in Rio, they were approaching five hours late. Unbelievably, the band were able to take to the stage on time at 10 p.m.; however, this was without any form of soundcheck. The video and audio recording equipment, which was only going to be used for this one night, had not been tested at all.

Amazingly, everything worked. Listeners may initially be shocked by the sheer audible volume of the crowd, who sound more akin to a football crowd than a rock audience. Their commitment to Rush is unequivocal however, loudly singing along to their favourite songs, as Peart remarks in the album's liner notes: 'That night's show had 40,000 stars.... Just listen to them singing along note-for-note with 'YYZ'—an instrumental—and you realize this is no ordinary audience'.

Rush in Rio is the first Rush live album to break the tradition of one live album after every four studio albums. The album also features an entire performance from one night of the tour. Previous albums had featured the best performances cherry-picked from several recorded performances. The album also includes the full, unabridged set: DVD and CD technology now gave the band flexibility to create an album that approaches three hours in length. The final oddity is the inclusion of an acoustic song. 'Resist' is performed by Lee and Lifeson on two acoustic guitars, giving Peart a break after his aerobic drum-solo.

R30

Released:	22 November 2005
Current edition:	Atlantic CD, Eagle Vision DVD/Blu-ray
Recorded at the Festhalle, Frankfurt	
On-site audio producer:	François Lamoureux
Chart positions:	None

With *Rush in Rio* and *Different Stages* providing a record of the band's prior two tours, many did not see a necessity for yet another live release. Nevertheless, one night of the hugely successful *R30* tour was recorded for posterity. This tour commemorated the thirtieth anniversary of the formation of the definitive Rush line-up.

While planning the route for the *Vapor Trails* tour, Peart described the difficulty the band found in sating their growing demand as a touring act, while still giving themselves some time away from work: 'Europe continued to hang like an unanswered question, for we hadn't toured over there for ten years'— while the *Vapor Trails* tour did ultimately leave European fans disappointed, the *R30* tour thrilled fans in over a dozen European cities, with the Frankfurt show being used for the release.

Several songs that were also played on the *Vapor Trails* tour were not included on the *R30* release in order to avoid numerous duplicates, but *R30* does have its unique moments. The hugely popular opener the 'R30 Overture'—a medley of six carefully segued early Rush songs—was received by fans with enthusiastic fervour.

Some odd decisions were associated with the album: 'Animate' is significantly slower and inexplicably loses the second half of its first verse, there is the bizarre 'party dragon' motif, and, of course, the apparently acquisitive decision to release another live album less than two years after their last. Thus, fans approached the new release with some cynicism. The release was, however, extremely successful, and is yet another record of Rush's enormously powerful live presence. While *Rush in Rio* was a defiant performance, triumphing over adversity, *R30* was the band more confident and honed than ever.

Snakes and Arrows Live

Released: 14 April 2008
Current edition: Atlantic CD, Eagle Vision DVD/Blu-ray
Recorded at Ahoy Arena, Rotterdam
On site Audio Producer: François Lamoureux, assisted by Brian Mercier
Chart positions: Canada: 8
                           UK: 70
                           US: 18

Recorded over two nights at Rotterdam's Ahoy arena, *Snakes and Arrows Live*, like the band's two previous live albums, is the soundtrack to the concert video of the same name.

Back on the road as a working band, Rush make no apologies for the copious volume of new material included on this latest live album; with nine of the studio album's thirteen tracks included on this wide-ranging double album. While some detractors criticised the band for releasing yet another live album, many fans were quick to praise the band for continuing to perform new material rather than just going over their greatest hits.

The performance is typically energetic and impressively proficient, although Rush's reputation for such performances means that anything less than this would have been met with derision. However, Lee's voice was, at this time, showing some of the first signs of age with his mid to high register beginning to weaken. Owing to this, the band had begun to slightly drop the tuning of some of their early material, with 'Circumstances' being down-tuned by a whole tone on this release.

The album was mixed by Richard Chycki and Alex Lifeson, while Hugh Syme provided the artwork.

Grace Under Pressure Live

Released: 11 August 2009
Current edition: Universal CD
Recorded at Maple Leaf Gardens Toronto, 1984

Stereo mix by Mike Fraser and Alex Lifeson
Assistant engineers: Zach Blackstone, Andrew Bigham
Audio Director: Bill Barker
Chart positions: None

This live album is the soundtrack to a video that was first released in 1984. This energetic performance was recorded at Maple Leaf Gardens in Toronto. The hometown show surges with energy throughout, and while the sound quality is not necessarily up to the standard of some of the band's other live releases, it is an interesting record of the band as they were in the mid-'80s. The audio album was anachronistically released a quarter of a century after its recording and perhaps represents the continuing trend of the band's management to capitalise on any available live recordings. While many considered the audio release of this relic unnecessary, it is an entertaining album and a good live representation of the band in their synthesizer heyday.

Time Machine 2011: Live in Cleveland

Released: 8 November 2011
Current edition: Roadrunner CD, Anthem DVD
Recorded at Quicken Loans Arena, Cleveland, Ohio
Recording engineers: Richard Chycki, Joel Singer
Mixed by Richard Chycki
Charted: Canada: 59
                         UK: 70
                         US: 54

More than thirty years after Cleveland's appreciation for 'Working Man' helped to launch the band's career, Rush honoured the city with a live release recorded there.

The *Time Machine* tour (2011) saw Rush perform their 1981 album *Moving Pictures* live in full. While the tour was unquestionably nostalgic, the band were able to pre-emptively silence their critics by including three new pieces that had, at this point, not been included on any Rush album. 'BU2B' and 'Caravan' had been released as singles before the tour and would subsequently be included on the band's *Clockwork Angels* album, while Lifeson's short acoustic introduction to 'Closer to the Heart'; 'O'Malley's Break' is only available on this release.

While many of this album's tracks have been included on live releases before, many fans were thrilled at the opportunity of having an officially sanctioned, high-quality recording of Rush performing 'The Camera Eye' live. This song, which the band had fallen out of love with in later years, was one of the most requested songs for the band to perform live after it was dropped from their set in the mid-'80s.

While the tour and live release were widely praised, Lee's vocal performance was heavily criticised, with many drawing attention to straining, poor diction, and occasional false notes. While Lee has suffered criticism for his singing from the very beginning of Rush's career, it was at around this point that many genuine fans began to voice their concerns, urging the band to consider down-tuning their entire set and dropping altogether some of the band's earlier, more vocally challenging material.

The tour and its accompanying releases are stylised with 'steampunk' imagery and motifs. This world of futuristic steam-machinery would go on to become a huge part of the band's next studio release, *Clockwork Angels*.

Like its predecessor, this live album was, once again, mixed by Richard Chycki

Clockwork Angels Live

Released: 19 November 2013
Current edition: streaming audio only
Recorded at Phoenix, Arizona; Dallas, Texas; San Antonio, Texas
Recording engineers: Richard Chycki, Joel Singer
Mixed by Mike Fraser
Clockwork Angels String Ensemble:
Conductor: David Campbell
Violins: Mario De Leon, Joel Derouin, Jonathan Dinklage, Gerry Hilera, Audrey Solomon, Hiroko Taguchi, Entcho Todorov
Cellos: Adele Stein, Jacob Szekely
Chart positions: Canada: 75
UK: 65
US: 33

Had Rush continued with their tradition of releasing a live album after every fourth studio album, *Clockwork Angels Live* would have been the next release after *Different Stages*. This live release was unique at the time for its inclusion of additional live musicians. During the *Clockwork Angels* tour, the second half of the concert featured the band joined on stage by a nine-piece string section who helped to replicate the new album's string-heavy arrangements. Never a band to shy away from performing their new material, this live release includes no less than ten tracks from *Clockwork Angels*: the entire album but for 'BU2B' and 'BU2B2'.

Recorded in Dallas, Phoenix, and San Antonio, *Clockwork Angels Live* features highlights of three nights on the band's highly successful tour. During this tour, the band rotated the set list in order to feature a variety of different songs—four 'bonus' tracks that would ordinarily have been featured in the main set, depending on the night, are included at the end of this triple-disc release.

As well as the considerable number of *Clockwork Angels* tracks, this album includes a surprisingly large number of rarities, specifically from the band's 1980s electronic period. As well as songs from *Signals*, *Grace Under Pressure*, and *Hold Your Fire*, this album includes five tracks from 1985's *Power Windows*, a wonderful surprise for fans of this sometimes overlooked album.

While no Rush show would be complete without a drum solo, this tour featured Peart performing three solos. 'Here It Is!', the first solo, is performed as part of 'Where's My Thing'; 'Drumbastica' is a short but furiously energetic extension to 'Headlong Flight'; and 'The Percussor' is a two-part heavily electronic percussion solo.

Lifeson performs 'Peke's Repose', an unusual effect-laden acoustic intro to 'Halo Effect' that is not available on any other Rush album.

While many critics still found Lee's voice to be lacking on this release, it is hard to criticise a band who are still showing such ambition so far into their career. A confident set list of new tracks and rarities coupled with the unique inclusion of a string section on a Rush tour makes this unusual album an essential part of any Rush fan's collection.

R40 Live

Released: 20 November 2015
Current edition: Universal CD, Concord DVD / Blu-ray
Recorded at Air Canada Theatre, Toronto
Audio Producer: David Bottrill
Recorded and Mixed by David Bottrill
Additional musicians: Ben Mink and Jonathan Dinklage (violins on 'Losing It')
Chart positions: Canada: 30
UK: 47
US: 24

Forty-one years after the release of their debut album, Rush began their fortieth anniversary tour. *R40 Live* is mainly comprised of material from two nights at Toronto's Air Canada theatre, though recordings of six other songs that were not played in Toronto were recorded elsewhere and included on the final disc as bonus tracks.

Although it was never officially announced as such, the *R40* tour was thought by many to be an unofficial farewell tour. The show's first set began with material from *Clockwork Angels* and gradually moved backwards through time, both musically and visually. While the start of the show featured the full modern Rush setup, gradually the band's amplifiers, equipment, and lighting were altered as appropriate for the era of the material they were performing—the show finishes with amps placed on top of school-chairs as the enormous arena is turned into a high-school hall.

The second set included an entirely different drum kit, with Peart—to the delight of fans—appearing behind his double-kick drum setup—each emblazoned with *2112*'s 'star man' logo. In addition to the large electronic marimba, Peart also incorporated a set of tubular bells into this nostalgic setup.

Except for *Test for Echo*, *Presto*, *Hold Your Fire*, and *Power Windows*, each of Rush's original studio albums is represented in this wide-ranging set. Full of rarities, this live album finds the band performing material that had not been included in Rush's set for decades: 'Jacob's Ladder', parts of 'Cygnus X-1' (books one and two), and 'Lakeside Park' are songs that many believed would never be played live again. While many criticised some of Lee's arguably laboured vocals—particularly on material recorded in the band's early days—many relished the opportunity to see the band performing this rare material with the enthusiasm and excitement that it deserves. Perhaps most poignant is the inclusion of a song that the band had never played live before: 'Losing It'. Featuring the band's old friend Ben Mink on violin, the song is at once enthusing and heart-breaking. Rush—the band that never stopped moving forward—are finally saying goodbye. This tragic ode to the loss of greatness is given an emotional resonance by its composers, each now over sixty years old.

At the conclusion of the encore and with the last blast of 'Working Man' echoing throughout the hall, the band break into the riff from 'Garden Road', an early Rush song that was not included on their debut. The furious energy of their early days has been tempered by a sense of melody and a deeper understanding of song-writing, but if *R40* is Rush's swansong, it is undeniable that the band went out with a bang, and, most of all, in their own way, on their own terms.

Feedback—Covers Album

Release date: 29 June 2004
Current edition: Atlantic CD
Recorded at Phase One Studios, Toronto
Produced by David Leonard and Rush
Recorded by David Leonard
Mixed and Engineered by David Leonard
Phase One Pro Tools recording: Michael Jack assisted by Jeff Muir
Charted: Canada: 5
UK: 68
US: 19

The antithesis of the demanding and protracted *Vapor Trails* sessions two years prior, *Feedback* was a chance for Rush to re-engage with their early influences and enjoy the process of creating an album in the most organic and basic way. An album of eight cover versions, the most recent of which, 'The Seeker', was originally released in 1970, the oldest, Robert Johnson's 'Crossroads' (also known as 'Crossroad Blues') was first released in 1937.

Produced by David Leonard, who had recently worked on Lee's *My Favorite Headache*, *Feedback* suffers few, if any, of the production problems that plagued *Vapor Trails*. The simple approach of live-in-the-studio recording with minimal overdubs give the album an immediate and energetic sound; appropriately, most similar to Rush's early original releases. For those that were so disappointed with the sound of *Vapor Trails*, *Feedback* gave a glimmer of hope that the band were back on form and keen to return to the clarity and power that had characterised the majority of their previous albums.

Victor—Alex Lifeson Solo

Released: 9 January 1996
Current edition: Warner CD
Personnel: Alex Lifeson—spoken vocals, guitars, keyboards, bass, mandola, programming
Les Claypool—bass on 'The Big Dance'
Peter Cardinali—bass
Bill Bell—guitar
Dalbello—lead vocals on 'Start Today'
Edwin—lead vocals
Blake Manning—drums
Colleen Allen—horn
Charlene and Esther—spoken vocals on 'Shut Up Shuttin' Up'
Recorded at Lerxst Sound
Produced by Alex Lifeson
Chart positions: Canada: 71
UK: did not chart
US: 99

Advertised with the tag line 'Expect the Unexpected', *Victor* was a bizarre, exciting, and disturbing one-off album that Lifeson used as an outlet for his imitable hard rock guitar style, in addition to dark and electronic ambient pieces that would have little congruence with other Rush material. Lifeson produced and recorded the project himself at his home studio, Lerxst Sound, meaning that, at last, Lifeson's eccentricities could finally be received by the listener unadulterated.

While the album is, in essence, a solo project, Lifeson was careful to form a full band that functioned as such. Lifeson's decision to keep his name off the cover perhaps hindered sales, but the album itself is nevertheless an artistically honest, if complex, piece of work.

In addition to the core group, Primus bassist Les Claypool also makes a guest appearance on the album.

With its songs ranging from the Zappa-esque novelty track 'Shut Up Shuttin' Up' to the macabre spoken-word murder ballad of 'Victor' via the beautifully melodic instrumental 'Mr. X', *Victor* is an album of rarely paralleled variety. While it is often overlooked by even die-hard Rush fans, it documents one of Lifeson's proudest achievements as a recording artist.

Interesting Liner Notes

The album's cover features a collage of photographs from long-time Rush photographer Andrew MacNaughtan while the inlay, as well as a series of monochromatic photographs, features a grey-on-grey image of a rose, indicative of the album's main lyrical theme: the dark side of love.

Special thanks are offered to 'nobody in particular', while grateful acknowledgements for technical assistance are offered to, among numerous firms, 'The Omega Concern'. This company was formed by Lifeson as a small design and engineering company, primarily to manufacture his own design of guitar-performer stand. This stand holds an acoustic guitar in playing position in order that Lifeson can quickly switch from acoustic to electric.

The album is dedicated to Lifeson's wife, Charlene, 'for her inspiration, spirit and loving support'.

My Favorite Headache—Geddy Lee Solo

Released:	14 November 2000
Current edition:	Not currently available
Personnel:	Geddy Lee—bass guitar, vocals, guitar, piano, programming, percussion, string arrangements, producer, engineer
	Ben Mink—guitars, violins, violas, programming, string arrangements, producer, engineer
	Matt Cameron—drums
	Jeremy Taggart—drums on 'Home on the Strange'
	John Friesen—cellos on 'Working at Perfekt'
	Ed Wilson—additional programming

Chris Stringer—additional percussion
Waylon Wall—steel guitar on 'Window to the World'
Pappy Rosen—backing vocals on 'Slipping'

Recorded at The Peasant's Tent and Reaction Studios, Toronto; East and West and The Factory Studios, Vancouver, British Columbia; Studio X, Seattle, Washington and Metalworks Studios, Mississauga, Ontario.

Produced by Geddy Lee, Bink Mink and David Leonard

Engineered by Adam Kasper, Dennis Tougas

Assistant engineers: Sam Hofstedt, Sheldon Zaharko, Chris Stringer, Tom Heron, Jeff Elliot, Joel Kazmi, Ian Bodzasi

Chart positions: Canada: did not chart
UK: did not chart
US: 52

Released four years after what, at the time, was believed by many to be Rush's final studio album, *My Favourite Headache* provided some musical nourishment to the enormous number of Rush fans who were eager for more musical output from Lee, Lifeson, and Peart.

Lee, who had never previously harboured any great desires to release a solo work, used the album as a repository for what would otherwise have been wasted creativity. All of Lee's previous musical work had been collaborative, and despite the album being a solo piece, the music was written by Lee in partnership with some-time Rush collaborator (and Lee's great friend), Ben Mink. Mink, well known as a violinist, also played the majority of guitars on the album.

While Lifeson's solo album *Victor* featured an enormous number of brilliantly off-the wall ideas executed in an, arguably, disorderly fashion, for *My Favorite Headache*, almost the opposite is true. Lee's talent as a songwriter is unarguable, and this album demonstrates excellent melodic sensitivity as well as lush and emotive harmonies; but the chaotic and haphazard influence of Lifeson is missing on tracks like 'Grace to Grace' that perhaps, otherwise, may have become classic Rush songs. The more delicate songs, such as 'Slipping' and 'Still', despite lacking the drive and excitement that many Rush fans love, are perhaps the most creatively successful of the album, with Lee expressing a previously unseen side of his songwriting.

The album's title comes from a favourite phrase of Mink's parents, as Lee recounts:

> Ben's dad was telling him a story about something that happened to his mother, and he said, in his Polish accent, 'and right away, she gets the favourite headache.' Once I stopped laughing, I realized what a great phrase that is, and I became determined to use it. It represents my sort of reluctant relationship with making music: I love it passionately, but it drives me crazy, because once I get into a project I'm completely consumed by it.[1]

Interesting Liner Notes

The abstract artwork was designed by Steve Mykolyn and Fuel Design Inc. while photographs were taken by Michael Graf and the ubiquitous Andrew MacNaughtan.

'THANKS AND I MEAN THANKS' are offered to 'Nancy Julian and Kyla for their encouragement, patience and patience!!' Lee acknowledges his bandmates, adding fuel to the fire of the rumours of a new Rush album: 'For their generosity of spirit ... (my soul brothers) Lerxst and Pratt!'

'Duke' is also credited for his role as 'Dog'.

Peart's Jazz Solos (Vapor Trails–Time Machine Tours)

Peart's solo 'O Baterista' is a traditional Peart solo in many respects, but for its finale, which features Peart performing over a backing track of the jazz number 'One O' Clock Jump' by Count Basie. Peart had performed drums on this track for the Buddy Rich Tribute *Burning for Buddy*. This drum solo would remain thematically similar for the next two tours, though the jazz finale would feature Duke Ellington's 'Cotton Tail' on the *Snakes and Arrows* tour and Cole Porter's 'Love for Sale' on the *Time Machine* tour. The titles 'O Baterista', 'Der Trommler', and 'De Slagwerker' all translate to 'The Drummer' in Portuguese, German, and Dutch respectively, while 'Moto Perpetuo' is a Latin term to describe a fast moving and changeable piece of music.

Endnotes

Chapter 1

1. James, B., 'Geddy Lee on 40 years of Rush', *The A.V. Club,* (www.music.avclub.com 4/12/2015).
2. Schroeder, A., 'Rush—Erwin Center, Sunday 12', *The Austin Chronicle,* p. 80 (6/10/2011).
3. Soeder, J., 'After Donna Halper gave "Working Man" a spin on WMMS, Rush's career took off', (www.cleveland.com 15/4/2011).

Chapter 2

1. Reed, R., 'HOW A "KINDA GOOFY" DRUMMER NAMED NEIL PEART MADE HIS WAY INTO RUSH', *Ultimate Classic Rock,* (www.ultimateclassicrock.com 29/7/2015).
2. Banasiewicz, B., *Rush Visions: The Official Biography* (United Kingdom: Omnibus Press 1990).

Chapter 3

1. Reed, R., 'WHEN RUSH DELVED INTO PROG WITH "CARESS OF STEEL"', *Ultimate Classic Rock,* (www.ultimateclassicrock.com 24/9/2015).
2. Author unknown, 'When Dream and Day Unite', Dream Theater Official Website (dreamtheater.net/discography).
3. Popoff, M., *Contents Under Pressure: 30 Years of Rush at Home and Away* (Google Books 2004).
4. Peart, N., *Traveling Music: The Soundtrack to My Life and Times* (ECW Press, Toronto, Canada, 2004).
5. Peart, N., 'Twenty-Five Questions An Interview with Neil Peart by You' *Rush Backstage Club Newsletter,* December 1985.
6. Peart, N., 'Rush—Roll The Bones', *Rush Backstage Club Newsletter,* October 1991.
7. Elliot, P., 'Heavy Load—Heavy questions for heavy rockers', *Classic Rock Magazine,* issue 190, p. 138 (Bath, Somerset, United Kingdom, Future Plc 2013).

Chapter 4

1. Popoff, M., *Contents Under Pressure: 30 Years of Rush at Home and Away* (Google Books 2004).
2. Miles, B., 'Is everybody feelin' all RIGHT? (Geddit...?)', *NME,* 4 March 1978, p. 7.
3. Peart, N., *Roadshow: Landscape with Drums: A Concert Tour by Motorcycle* (ECW Press, Toronto, Canada, 2011).

Endnotes

Chapter 5

1. Wilding, P., 'The masters of prog return!:—Grace Under Pressure', *Classic Rock Magazine*, October 2004 (Bath, Somerset, United Kingdom, Future Plc 2004).
2. Peart, N., with Lifeson, A., and Lee, G., *'A Condensed Rush Primer'* (Mercury Records, Chicago IL., USA, 1977).

Chapter 6

1. Iero, C., 'Neil Peart', *Modern Drummer*, April–May 1980, p. 13 (New Jersey, USA: Isabel Spagnardi 1980).
2. Welch, M., 'Neil Peart: Rand Paul 'hates women and brown people', *reason*, 16/6/2015 (www.reason.com 2015).
3. Unknown author, 'ABOUT HEMISPHERES', *Official Rush Website* (www.rush.com 2018).

Chapter 7

1. Simmons, S., 'The Moustache That Conquered The World', *Sounds Magazine*, 5/4/1980 (United Kingdom: United Newspapers 1980).
2. Mulhern, T., 'Alex Lifeson—Rush's Kinetic Lead Guitarist', *Guitar Player*, June 1980 (San Bruno, California, United States: Future Plc, 1980).
3. Peart, N., 'Twenty-Five Questions An Interview with Neil Peart by You', *Rush Backstage Club Newsletter*, December 1985.

Chapter 8

1. Popoff, M., *Rush—Updated Edition: The Unofficial Illustrated History* (Google Books 2016).
2. Bosso, J., 'Rush: Vital Signs', *Guitar World*, August 2007 (New York City, USA, Future US, Inc. 2007).
3. Leonard, M., 'Alex Lifeson in His Own Words', Gibson Official Website, 22/8/2014 (www.gibson.com 2014).
4. Radio Interview *'In The Studio with Redbeard'* Show #28 week of 2 January 1989 (Transcription available from www.2112.net).

Chapter 9

1. Hiatt, B., 'From Rush With Love', Rolling Stone Website, 16/6/2015 (www.rollingstone.com: Penske Media Corporation 2015).
2. Ling, D., 'The Albums That Saved PROG: Signals', *Prog*, vol. 43, February 2014, (Bath, Somerset, United Kingdom, Future Plc 2014).
3. Dome, M., 'Interview with Neil Peart', *Metal Hammer*, 25/4/1988, (United Kingdom, Future Publishing 1988).

Chapter 10

1. Podcast Interview 'Mohr Stories', *Steve Lillywhite VS. Jay Mohr on Mohr Stories 173* (Available on youtube.com).
2. Unnamed Correspondent, 'How the Holocaust rocked Rush front man Geddy Lee', *J. The Jewish News of Northern California*, 25/6/2004 (www.jweekly.com: San Francisco, USA).
3. Pollock, B., 'The Songwriting Interview: Neil Peart', *Guitar For The Practicing Musician*, October 1986 (Cherry Lane Music: United States 1986).

Chapter 11

1. Welch, E., 'RUSH Rocks To A Different Drummer', *The Boston Globe*, 5/12/1985, p. 118 (Boston, Massachusetts, USA, John W. Henry 1985).
2. Mulhern, T., 'Geddy Lee of Rush: Rock's Leading Bassist', *Guitar Player*, April 1986 (United States, Future Plc 1986).
3. Swenson, J., 'Geddy Lee Discusses the New Rush Album, *Power Windows*, in this 1986 Guitar World Interview', *Guitar World* (website) 8/9/2011 (www.guitarworld.com: New York City, USA, 2011).
4. Krewin, N., 'Surviving With Rush', *Canadian Composer*, April 1986 (Toronto, Canada, Société canadienne des auteurs, compositeurs et éditeurs de musique 1986).

Chapter 12

1. Peart, N., *Roadshow: Landscape with Drums: A Concert Tour by Motorcycle* (ECW Press, Toronto, Canada, 2011).
2. Greene, A., 'Flashback: Rush Team With Aimee Mann for Surreal "Time Stand Still" Video', *Rolling Stone Website*, 16/2/2017 (www.rollingstone.com: Penske Media Corporation 2015).
3. Ponting, T., 'Neil Peart: Mystic Rhythms', *Rhythm*, August 1988 (Bath, Somerset, United Kingdom, Future Plc: 1988).
4. Tannenbaum, R., 'Dear Superstar: Geddy Lee', *Blender*, April 2009 (New York, USA: Alpha Media Group 2009).
5. Peart, N., 'Rush—Roll The Bones', *Rush Backstage Club Newsletter*, October 1991.
6. Unknown author, 'Adventures in Paradise', *The National Midnight Star* (*Rush Fan Newsletter*), No. 481, 1/5/1992 (archived at www.white-barn.com/nms 1992).

Chapter 13

1. Dome, M., 'RUSH AND THE WEIRD RISE OF PROG METAL', *Metal Hammer*, March 2013 (United Kingdom, Future Publishing 2013).
2. Rush—Profiled Promotional Interview CD (Atlantic—PRCD 3200-2).
3. Popoff, M., *Contents Under Pressure: 30 Years of Rush at Home and Away* (Google Books 2004).
4. Dome, M., 'RUSH AND THE WEIRD RISE OF PROG METAL', *Metal Hammer*, March 2013 (United Kingdom, Future Publishing 2013).

Chapter 14

1. Peart, N., *Traveling Music: The Soundtrack to My Life and Times* (ECW Press, Toronto, Canada, 2004).
2. Widders-Ellis, A., 'Rush Redefined', *Guitar Player*, November 1991 (San Bruno, California, United States: Future Plc, 1991),

Chapter 15

1. Peart, N., 'A Port Boy's Story', *St. Catherine's Standard*, 24 & 25 June 1994 (St Catharines, Ontario: Metroland Media Group (Torstar) 1994).

Chapter 16

1. Myers, P., 'Rush Put Themselves To The "Test" (And End Up Even Closer To The Heart)', December 1996 (Niagara Falls, Ontario, Canada: Norris-Whitney Communications Inc. 1996).

2. Sakamoto, J., 'Ready To Test Echo On The Road', *Jam!Showbiz*, 16/10/1996 (Toronto, Canada: Postmedia Network 1996).
3. Streeter, S., 'The Steve Streeter and Neil Peart Interview', *A Show Of Fans*, No. 17, Summer 1997 (Rush fan-zine—transcription available from www.2112.net 1997).

Chapter 17

1. Daly, S., 'Alex Lifeson Interview: Rush's Axeman Looks Back and Moves Forward', *Guitar International* (guitarinternational.com—article undated).
2. Peart, N. 'The Making of Vapor Trails' *Vapor Trails Tourbook* (Anthem Entertainment 2002).
3. Coburn, B., 'Rockline 25/5/2002', *Radio Interview*, (Los Angeles, California, USA 2002).
4. Unknown author, 'VAPOR TRAILS REMIXED', *www.rush.com*, press release 1/8/2013 (Anthem Entertainment 2013).

Chapter 18

1. Peart, N. 'Snakes and Arrows Live' *Snakes and Arrows Tourbook* (Anthem Entertainment 2008)
2. *Ibid.*
3. 'The Game of Snakes and Arrows' Documentary (Anthem Entertainment 2007)
4. Peart, N., *Traveling Music: The Soundtrack to My Life and Times* (ECW Press, Toronto, Canada, 2004)
5. Peart, N., 'The Game of Snakes and Arrows: Prize Every Time' *Essay* (Promotional Essay 2007)
6. 'The Game of Snakes and Arrows' Documentary (Anthem Entertainment 2007)
7. Peart, N., 'The Game of Snakes and Arrows: Prize Every Time' *Essay* (Promotional Essay 2007)

Chapter 19

1. Giles, J., 'RUSH—2012 NEW ALBUM PREVIEW', *Ultimate Classic Rock*, 3/1/2012 (Greenwich, Connecticut, USA, Townsquare Media Group 2012).
2. Bosso, J., 'Interview: producer Nick Raskulinecz on Rush's Clockwork Angels', musicradar.com, 11/6/2012 (Bath, Somerset, UK, Future Plc 2012).
3. Peart, N., 'The Future As Seen From The Past or: "Yesterday's Tomorrowland"', *Clockwork Angels Tourbook* (Anthem Entertainment 2012).
4. *Ibid.*
5. Press release: 'Rush Announces Clockwork Angels Tour', *PRNewswire*, 19/4/2012 (New York, USA 2012).
6. Bosso, J., 'Interview: Alex Lifeson talks Rush's Clockwork Angels track-by-track', musicradar.com, 25/5/2012 (Bath, Somerset, UK, Future Plc 2012).
7. *Ibid.*
8. Peart, N., 'The Future As Seen From The Past or: "Yesterday's Tomorrowland"', *Clockwork Angels Tourbook* (Anthem Entertainment 2012).

Chapter 20

1. Jisi, C., 'NO RUSH: GEDDY LEE FLEXES HIS MUSCLES IN A POWERFUL SOLO DEBUT'.

Bibliography

Author unknown, 'When Dream and Day Unite', Dream Theater Official Website (dreamtheater.net/discography)
Banasiewicz, B., *Rush Visions: The Official Biography* (United Kingdom: Omnibus Press 1990)
Bass Player Magazine, January 2001 (San Bruno, California, USA, Future Plc 2001)
Bosso, J., 'Rush: Vital Signs', *Guitar World*, August 2007 (New York City, USA, Future US, Inc. 2007)
Bosso, J., 'Interview: Alex Lifeson talks Rush's Clockwork Angels track-by-track', *musicradar. com* 25/5/2012 (Bath, Somerset, UK, Future Plc 2012)
Bosso, J., 'Interview: producer Nick Raskulinecz on Rush's Clockwork Angels' *musicradar. com* 11/6/2012 (Bath, Somerset, UK, Future Plc 2012)
Coburn, B., 'Rockline 25/5/2002', *Radio Interview,* (Los Angeles, California, USA 2002)
Daly, S., 'Alex Lifeson Interview: Rush's Axeman Looks Back and Moves Forward', *Guitar International* (guitarinternational.com—article undated)
Dome, M., 'Interview with Neil Peart', *Metal Hammer*, 25/4/1988, (United Kingdom, Future Publishing 1988)
Dome, M., 'RUSH AND THE WEIRD RISE OF PROG METAL', *Metal Hammer*, March 2013 (United Kingdom, Future Publishing 2013)
Elliot, P., 'Heavy Load—Heavy questions for heavy rockers', *Classic Rock Magazine,* issue 190, p. 138 (Bath, Somerset, United Kingdom, Future Plc 2013)
Giles, J., 'RUSH—2012 NEW ALBUM PREVIEW', *Ultimate Classic Rock* 3/1/2012 (Greenwich, Connecticut, USA, Townsquare Media Group 2012)
Greene, A., 'Flashback: Rush Team With Aimee Mann for Surreal "Time Stand Still" Video', *Rolling Stone Website* 16/2/2017 (www.rollingstone.com: Penske Media Corporation 2015)
Hiatt, B., 'From Rush With Love', *Rolling Stone Website,* 16/6/2015 (www.rollingstone.com: Penske Media Corporation 2015)
Iero, C., 'Neil Peart', *Modern Drummer,* April–May 1980; p. 13 (New Jersey, USA: Isabel Spagnardi 1980)
James, B., 'Geddy Lee on 40 years of Rush', *The A.V. Club,* (www.music.avclub.com 4/12/2015)
Jisi, C., 'NO RUSH: GEDDY LEE FLEXES HIS MUSCLES IN A POWERFUL SOLO DEBUT', *Bass Player Magazine* January 2001 (San Bruno, California, USA, Future Plc 2001)
Krewin, N., 'Surviving With Rush', *Canadian Composer,* April 1986 (Toronto, Canada, Société canadienne des auteurs, compositeurs et éditeurs de musique 1986)
Leonard, M., 'Alex Lifeson in His Own Words', Gibson Official Website 22/8/2014 (www. gibson.com 2014)

Bibliography

Ling, D., 'The Albums That Saved PROG: Signals', *Prog*, vol. 43, February 2014, (Bath, Somerset, United Kingdom, Future Plc 2014)

Miles, B., 'Is everybody feelin' all RIGHT? (Geddit...?)', *NME*, 4 March 1978, p. 7

Mulhern, T., 'Alex Lifeson—Rush's Kinetic Lead Guitarist', *Guitar Player*, June 1980 (San Bruno, California, United States: Future Plc, 1980)

Mulhern, T., 'Geddy Lee of Rush: Rock's Leading Bassist', *Guitar Player*, April 1986 (United States, Future Plc 1986)

Myers, P., 'Rush Put Themselves To The "Test" (And End Up Even Closer To The Heart)', December 1996 (Niagara Falls, Ontario, Canada: Norris-Whitney Communications Inc. 1996)

Peart, N., 'Snakes and Arrows Live' *Snakes and Arrows Tourbook* (Anthem Entertainment 2008)

Peart, N., 'The Making of Vapor Trails' *Vapor Trails Tourbook* (Anthem Entertainment 2002)

Peart, N., with Lifeson, A., and Lee, G., 'A Condensed Rush Primer' (Mercury Records, Chicago IL., USA, 1977)

Peart, N., 'A Port Boy's Story', *St. Catherine's Standard* 24 & 25th June, 1994 (St Catharine's, Ontario: Metroland Media Group (Torstar) 1994)

Peart, N., *Roadshow: Landscape with Drums: A Concert Tour by Motorcycle* (ECW Press, Toronto, Canada, 2011)

Peart, N., 'Rush—Roll The Bones', *Rush Backstage Club Newsletter*, October 1991

Peart, N., 'The Future As Seen From The Past or: "Yesterday's Tomorrowland" *Clockwork Angels Tourbook* (Anthem Entertainment 2012)

Peart, N., 'The Game of Snakes and Arrows: Prize Every Time' *Essay* (Promotional Essay 2007)

Peart, N., *Traveling Music: The Soundtrack to My Life and Times* (ECW Press, Toronto, Canada, 2004)

Peart, N., 'Twenty-Five Questions An Interview with Neil Peart by You', *Rush Backstage Club Newsletter*, December 1985

Podcast Interview 'Mohr Stories' *Steve Lillywhite VS. Jay Mohr on Mohr Stories 173* (Available on youtube.com)

Pollock, B., 'The Songwriting Interview: Neil Peart', *Guitar For The Practicing Musician*, October 1986 (Cherry Lane Music: United States 1986)

Ponting, T., 'Neil Peart: Mystic Rhythms', *Rhythm*, August 1988 (Bath, Somerset, United Kingdom, Future Plc: 1988)

Popoff, M., *Contents Under Pressure: 30 Years of Rush at Home and Away* (Google Books 2004)

Popoff, M., *Rush—Updated Edition: The Unofficial Illustrated History* (Google Books 2016)

Press Release: 'Rush Announces Clockwork Angels Tour' *PRNewswire* 19/4/2012 (New York, USA 2012)

Radio Interview *'In The Studio with Redbeard'* Show #28 week of 2 January 1989 (Transcription available from www.2112.net)

Reed, R., 'HOW A "KINDA GOOFY" DRUMMER NAMED NEIL PEART MADE HIS WAY INTO RUSH', *Ultimate Classic Rock*, (www.ultimateclassicrock.com 29/7/2015)

Reed, R., 'WHEN RUSH DELVED INTO PROG WITH 'CARESS OF STEEL', *Ultimate Classic Rock*, (www.ultimateclassicrock.com 24/9/2015)

Rush—Profiled Promotional Interview CD (Atlantic—PRCD 3200-2)

Sakamoto, J., 'Ready To Test Echo On The Road', *Jam!Showbiz*, 16/10/1996 (Toronto, Canada: Postmedia Network 1996)

Schroeder, A., 'Rush—Erwin Center, Sunday 12', *The Austin Chronicle*, p. 80 (6/10/2011)

Simmons, S., 'The Moustache That Conquered The World', *Sounds Magazine*, 5/4/1980 (United Kingdom: United Newspapers 1980)

Soeder, J., 'After Donna Halper gave "Working Man" a spin on WMMS, Rush's career took off', (www.cleveland.com 15/4/2011)

Streeter S., 'The Steve Streeter And Neil Peart Interview' *A Show Of Fans* #17, Summer 1997 (Rush fan-zine—transcription available from www.2112.net 1997)

Swenson, J., 'Geddy Lee Discusses the New Rush Album, *Power Windows*, in this 1986 Guitar World Interview', *Guitar World* (website) 8/9/2011 (www.guitarworld.com: New York City, USA, 2011)

Tannenbaum, R., 'Dear Superstar: Geddy Lee', *Blender*, April 2009 (New York, USA: Alpha Media Group 2009)

The Game of Snakes and Arrows Documentary (Anthem Entertainment 2007)

Unknown author, 'VAPOR TRAILS REMIXED' www.rush.com press release 1/8/2013 (Anthem Entertainment 2013)

Unknown author, 'ABOUT HEMISPHERES', *Official Rush Website* (www.rush.com 2018)

Unknown author, 'Adventures in Paradise', *The National Midnight Star* (*Rush Fan Newsletter*), No. 481, 1/5/1992 (archived at www.white-barn.com/nms 1992)

Unnamed Correspondent, 'How the Holocaust rocked Rush front man Geddy Lee', *J. The Jewish News of Northern California*, 25/6/2004 (www.jweekly.com: San Francisco, USA)

Welch, E., 'RUSH Rocks To A Different Drummer', *The Boston Globe*, 5/12/1985, p. 118 (Boston, Massachusetts, USA, John W. Henry 1985)

Welch, M., 'Neil Peart: Rand Paul 'hates women and brown people', *reason*, 16/6/2015 (www.reason.com 2015)

Widders-Ellis, A., 'Rush Redefined', *Guitar Player*, November 1991 (San Bruno, California, United States: Future Plc, 1991)

Wilding, P., 'The masters of prog return!:—Grace Under Pressure', *Classic Rock Magazine*, October 2004 (Bath, Somerset, United Kingdom, Future Plc 2004)